110650041

On Tiptoe with
LOVE

ON TIPTOE
WITH
Love

*"Where the Holy Spirit is,
there is love."*

by

John T. Seamands

BEACON HILL PRESS OF KANSAS CITY
Kansas City, Missouri

Preface

"What the world needs now is love, sweet love," is the punch line of a popular song we have been hearing on the radio and television recently. The song is true. What the world needs is a giant dose of love.

A basic question is, "What kind of love does the world need?"

Much is said about love these days. Novel after novel has been written, song after song composed, movie after movie produced with love as the theme. And yet people know less about true love than ever before. Love has lost its character, its content. The very *word* "love" stands in need of redemption.

Another important question is, "Where will we find this love?"

Men are seeking everywhere for love. Some seek it in our universities, in our homes, in our churches. Others seek it in nightclubs, in love-ins, in and out of marriage. And yet we are finding less and less of true love than ever before. There is bitterness, hatred, abuse, rancor, and violence on every hand. Love itself has turned to lust.

The Bible has much to say about love. "God is love" . . . "Christ loved" . . . "The fruit of the Spirit is love" . . . "Love God with all your heart, mind, soul, and strength" . . . "Love your neighbor as yourself" . . . "Love your enemies." True love is Christlike. It is pure, unselfish, sacrificial. True love is God-given. It is poured into our hearts by the Holy Spirit, who is granted to us.

If we want to know the true meaning of love—if we want to find genuine, eternal love, we must get back to God. God is the Source of love. Christ is the supreme demonstration of love. The Holy Spirit enables us to love.

Jesus said to His disciples, "By this all men will know that you are my disciples, if you have love for one another." It was said of the early Christians, "Behold, how these people love one another!"

It is not enough to say to the world, "God is love." People must see this love. The disciples of Christ must show it to them. And the only way to demonstrate love is first to receive it from God through the indwelling presence of His Spirit. The Spirit-filled life is thus the secret of a genuine life of love, for love is the fruit of the Spirit. Therefore we do not seek love by itself, but we seek the Holy Spirit, who is the Source of love. Where the Spirit is, there is love.

JOHN T. SEAMANDS

Contents

1
Living Below Par

Recently in Hollywood, Fla., an elderly woman suddenly passed away. Her husband had been a lawyer in one of the New England states and upon his death she had moved to Florida. She dressed shabbily and lived alone in an old, ramshackle house. In sympathy the neighbors often picked her up in their cars and took her to the supermarket or out for an evening drive. Once a week a maid came and helped her clean the house.

One day when the maid entered the house, she found the lady dead in her bed. The maid immediately informed the police, and while they were inspecting the house, they found approximately a million dollars in currency, stuffed away in old shoe boxes and cartons. Upon further investigation they discovered that she had a savings account in the bank with almost another million dollars.

Since the widow's death was sudden, an autopsy was ordered by the police. Imagine the surprise of all when the diagnosis was made known. Malnutrition!

The story is told of a young Irishman who, many years ago, decided to migrate to the New World to make his way in life. He worked hard in his homeland until he had just enough money to purchase his steamship ticket across the

Atlantic. With the little bit of change that remained, he bought some biscuits and a can of cheese, which he intended to use for his meals on board ship. So for several days at sea, at mealtime the Irishman went down to his cabin and ate his cheese and biscuits. But soon the salt air made the biscuits soggy and the cheese hard, and the young man became tired of this meager fare.

One noon he was sitting in his cabin, hungry and feeling sorry for himself, when a steward passed by the open door carrying a tray with a delicious-looking meal. He beckoned the waiter and asked him, "Sir, tell me, where can I get a good meal like that?"

"How did you get on board ship?" asked the waiter. "Don't you have a ticket?"

"Certainly I have a ticket," replied the young passenger.

The waiter looked at the Irishman in astonishment. "Sir, don't you realize that your ticket entitles you to all your meals on board ship? You can go to the dining room, order anything you want on the menu, and eat as much as you like."

Here the young man was existing on biscuits and cheese, when he could have been feasting all along!

Many Christians are like the elderly lady in Florida and the young immigrant from Ireland. They are living far below their spiritual resources and privileges. They are without joy, when God offers them "joy unspeakable and full of glory." They are without peace, when God wants to give them "peace . . . which passes all understanding." They are defeated and discouraged, when God wants them to be "more than conquerors" through Christ, the all-victorious One. They are fruitless and ineffective, when the Heavenly Father wants to endue them with "power from on high," so that they may bear much fruit.

In Jesus' parable of the prodigal son, the elder brother was quite indignant when he heard the news from one of the servants that his brother had returned home from the far country and his father was providing a feast for him. He reacted in jealousy and self-pity and refused to enter the house. His father had to come out and entreat him to join the party. Note the force of the dialogue that followed:

The elder son said: "These many years I have served you, and I never disobeyed your command; yet you never gave me a kid, that I might make merry with my friends. But when this son of yours came, who has devoured your living with harlots, you killed for him the fatted calf!"

The father calmly replied: "Son, you are always with me, and all that is mine is yours."

The elder son could have had many a feast. But he didn't have, because he didn't ask. He never claimed his possessions.

The Heavenly Father is saying to us today, "All that I have is yours. All My resources are at your disposal." If we are not living the abundant life, it is simply because we have not claimed our full inheritance in Christ. Jesus said that the Heavenly Father will "give the Holy Spirit to those that ask Him" (Luke 11:13).

Jesus spoke of the Gift of the Holy Spirit as *the promise of the Father*. God had given many promises to His children. We have lifted them out of the Old and New Testaments and have put them into mottoes on our walls. We sing them in our hymns; we memorize them; we treasure them in our hearts. But Jesus picked out this promise and called it *"the promise of the Father."* Of all the promises the Father gave, this is *the* promise. Why? Because all the other promises He gave were usually about gifts—the gift of peace, of comfort, of guidance, of sustenance. But here was the promise of the Gift of the Giver. The Giver was giving himself, and there was nothing higher He could give.

In the giving of the Holy Spirit, the Father was giving just that—himself. No wonder it was *the* promise. This focused all the scattered promises into one. The gifts became one—the Giver! It is like the lover who has given many gifts to his intended bride—candy, perfume, flowers. But now he comes to the sacred marriage day, when he gives the final gift—himself. It is *the* gift. Without that all the other gifts would be bare. The gift of himself consummates all the gifts. Likewise the Heavenly Father, having given many gifts to His children, comes now to the consummating moment, the moment of giving himself to the receptive one. If we miss this, we miss God's greatest Gift.

The Apostle Paul describes the gift of the Holy Spirit as "the guarantee of our inheritance until we acquire possession of it" (Eph. 1:14). The Greek word for "guarantee" is *arrabōn,* which literally means "down payment." The *arrabōn* was a regular feature of the Greek business world. It was a part of the purchase price of anything paid in advance as a guarantee that the rest of the price would in due time be paid. If a person sold a cow, he received so many drachmas as *arrabōn,* that is, as surety that the full price would duly be paid. If someone hired a group of entertainers, he paid so much in advance as a guarantee that the remainder of the money would be paid and the contract be honored after the performance had been given.

When I went to India as a young missionary I soon learned the meaning of a "down payment" or "advance." Whenever I called a carpenter or mason or coolie to do some job around the house, first we bargained about the total cost of the materials and labor. When this was agreed upon, the laborer always asked for a "down payment." For example, if the estimate came to 50 rupees, the man would ask for about five or 10 rupees as an advance. This sealed the bargain and made the contract valid. When the laborer completed the work, the balance of the amount was paid.

So what Paul is saying is that the experience of the Holy Spirit which we have in this world is a foretaste of the joys and blessedness of heaven; it is the guarantee that someday we will enter into the fullness of our inheritance in Christ.

Suppose a lawyer unexpectedly called on you and said: "Sir, you have a rich uncle who died recently in South Africa and left his entire estate to you. I have been appointed as executor of the will. Your uncle was a very wealthy man and owned vast shares in a diamond mine, a gold mine, and a uranium mine. Now it will take several months to settle the whole estate, but in the meantime if you are in need of some money, I'll be glad to give you an advance *[arrabōn]* to help you out."

Immediately you say to yourself, This is great. I could use a few hundred dollars to buy the family some clothes or make some repairs on the house. You say to the lawyer, "Yes, Sir, I'll be happy to receive a small down payment. How much can you give?"

The lawyer says, "How would it be if I gave you a check now for $500,000? Would that help out?"

You can hardly believe your ears. "Did you say five thousand or five *hundred* thousand?"

"I said $500,000," replies the lawyer. "I'm sorry it's such a small amount."

"Small amount! How much then is the whole estate worth?"

"Oh, Sir, it's far more than I can describe. It's beyond one's imagination."

When Paul speaks of the Gift of the Holy Spirit as the *arrabōn,* the down payment of our final inheritance, he is emphasizing the profound truth that the greatest and most intimate experience of Christian peace and joy which is possible in this life is only a faint foretaste of the joy into which we shall one day enter. It is as if God said to us when He accepts us as His children, "Son, Daughter, I can't usher you into My presence just now, for I have a task for you to perform on earth. But I'll do the next best thing. I'll give you My presence in the person of the holy Spirit, and He will abide with you day and night, in sickness and in health, in joy and in sorrow. I can't bring you up into heaven right away, but I'll put a little bit of heaven inside of you. This will be a foretaste of what is yet to come."

"Lord, it's so wonderful to have You living in our hearts through the Holy Spirit and to know that You are with us at all times. It's so marvelous to experience Your joy and peace amidst all the trials and sorrows of life. If this is just a foretaste of heaven, what must the final inheritance be like?"

God offers the fullness of the Holy Spirit and the abundant life to all His children. Have we claimed our inheritance? Are we living up to our resources?

2

Where Was He Before?

The last words of our parting loved ones are the most treasured and most heeded.

For many years I have kept within the pages of my Bible a little scrap of paper on which my precious grandmother scribbled her parting message to me before her death in November, 1943. Grandmother was very dear to my brother and me. She became a widow at the age of 47, and then when she was 55 years of age she moved her residence to India in order to make a home for the two of us to attend school in the city while our parents were engaged in missionary work in the interior. Later she moved to Wilmore, Ky., to keep house for my brother and me as we attended Asbury Academy and Asbury College respectively. Grandmother financed all our musical training and presented each of us with a piano, a trombone, and an accordion. So she was very much like a second mother to us.

Grandmother had suffered a serious heart attack at her home in Kentucky, and realizing that death was near, she sent the following message to me as a young missionary in India:

> My darling J. T. This is good-bye. I'm going to be with Jesus. Your little Sylvia [our year-old daughter] is so sweet. Preach the Word and stick to the old Book. Be a good boy and meet me in heaven.
>
> Love, *Grandma*

This was Grandmother's last message to me, so I have guarded it carefully down through the years. I have earnestly sought to preach the Word. Someday I intend to meet her in heaven.

Now if we treasure and respect so highly the last words of our earthly loved ones, how much more should we give attention to the last words of our divine Saviour and Lord!

What were the last words of Jesus to His disciples before He ascended to the Father? He had said many deathless things to them—"Love your enemies . . . Be the servant of all . . . Lose your life in order to find it," etc. But what did He pick out as of the greatest importance? The last thing of which He would speak? Note these two passages penned by Luke, the early Christian historian.

> *Behold, I send the promise of my Father upon you; but stay in the city, until you are clothed with power from on high. Then he led them out as far as Bethany, and lifting up his hands he blessed them. While he blessed them, he parted from them* (Luke 24:49-50).
> *And while staying with them he charged them not to depart from Jerusalem, but to wait for the promise of the Father, which, he said, "you heard from me, for John baptized with water, but before many days you shall be baptized with the Holy Spirit." ". . . you shall receive power when the Holy Spirit has come upon you; and you shall be my witnesses . . ." And when he said this, as they were looking on, he was lifted up, and a cloud took him out of their sight* (Acts 1:4-5, 8-9).

Thus the last words of Jesus to His disciples were concerning the Holy Spirit. Jesus knew that if they missed this truth they would miss the whole point of redemption. For the Holy Spirit is Redemption—continuing Redemption within us. Apart from Him, redemption is outside of us—in history, in the historical Jesus. But through the Holy Spirit the historical becomes personal; through Him the divine incarnation becomes the divine inhabitation.

So Jesus commanded His disciples not to depart from

Jerusalem, but to wait for the enduement of power from on high through the fullness of the Holy Spirit.

During His earthly ministry Jesus uttered three important words. At the beginning of His ministry He said, "*Come*"—"Come to me, all who labor and are heavy laden" (Matt. 11:28). After His resurrection He commanded His disciples to "*Go*"—"Go therefore and make disciples of all nations" (Matt. 28:19). And just before His ascension He commanded them to "*Tarry*"—Tarry "in the city, until you are clothed with power from on high" (Luke 24:49). It is the tarrying that makes the coming and going effectual.

As in each case, along with the command Jesus gave His disciples a promise. When He said, "Come," He promised, "I will give you rest." When He commanded them to "go," He promised, "Lo, I will be with you always." And when He commanded them to "tarry," He promised, "You shall be baptized with the Holy Spirit . . . you shall receive power."

What was the response of the disciples to Jesus' final command? In the first place, they responded with *obedience*. They immediately returned to Jerusalem and went to the Upper Room. They made no detours; they wasted no time. The Master had said, "Tarry," and, "Receive," so they were determined in their hearts to tarry until they received the Gift of the Holy Spirit. All other plans and duties were laid aside for the moment. There was only one item of business on the agenda. Christ's command took precedence over everything else.

If we Christians today are to be effective instruments of redemption and reconciliation in a world of turmoil and tension, we will have to take seriously the injunction of our Lord to tarry for the baptism with the Holy Spirit. We will have to be obedient to the exhortation. Peter made it clear that God gives the Holy Spirit "to them that obey him" (Acts 5:32). The command to tarry is just as much a command as the command to repent of our sins or to believe on the Lord

Jesus Christ. This is not something we can take or leave as we like. This is a must! For without the *fullness* of the Holy Spirit there can be no *usefullness.*

What would happen if the Church of today would momentarily push aside its building plans, its suppers and bazaars, its business meetings and financial drives, and just take time off to obey the Lord's command? We thrill at the very thought of it! It would probably spark one of the greatest revivals in history. Suppose the early disciples had not tarried for the enduement with power from on high. Would there be a Church today? Suppose we fail to tarry in our day. Will there be a Church tomorrow?

The record in Acts tells us that the disciples "with one accord devoted themselves to prayer" (Acts 1:14). They were not just gathered together in one place. They were of one heart and one mind. There was complete unity of purpose and desire. And they continued in prayer and supplication for several days, seeking for just one thing—the baptism with the Holy Spirit. Their prayers were all focused on this one objective.

The disciples not only responded to Christ's exhortation with obedience. They also responded with *faith.* They remembered the words of Jesus during His earthly ministry when He said, "If you then, who are evil, know how to give good gifts to your children, how much more will the heavenly Father give the Holy Spirit to *those who ask him!*" (Luke 11:13) Jesus had also said, "Ask, and it will be given you . . . For every one who asks receives" (Luke 11:9-10). Then, again, He had promised them just before His ascension that they would receive the baptism with the Holy Spirit in just a few days. So the disciples asked and in faith took Christ at His word that those who ask do receive. They let their whole weight down upon His promise. And the record tells us that on the Day of Pentecost "they were all filled with the Holy Spirit." The promise passed into fulfillment!

We must not make the mistake of thinking that the Holy Spirit first entered the world on the Day of Pentecost, that He was hiding behind the curtain all this time and then suddenly stepped onto the stage of human history. As God, He is coeternal with the Father and goes back to the beginning of time—yes, even before time. He has been at work in the world from the dawn of the universe.

In the Old Testament the Holy Spirit is referred to more than 90 times. He is most often designated as "the Spirit of the Lord" or "the Spirit of God." Many times He is simply referred to as "the Spirit." Three times He is called "the Holy Spirit." Occasionally He is referred to as the Spirit "of wisdom" or "of judgment" or "of grace."

The divine activity of the Holy Spirit is evident throughout the Old Testament. The Word reveals the fact that the Holy Spirit was an Agent in the creation of the universe. In Gen. 1:2 we read,"The earth was without form and void; and darkness was upon the face of the deep; and the Spirit of God was moving over the face of the waters." It was the Holy Spirit who brought order out of chaos. In another place we read that the Spirit "garnished the heavens" (Job 26:13, KJV).

The Holy Spirit was also active in the creation of man. Elihu, one of the main characters in the drama of Job, confessed this fact when he said, "The spirit of God hath made me, and the breath of the Almighty hath given me life" (Job 33:4, KJV). The Spirit also sustains all life upon this earth. Job said, "All the while my breath is in me, and the spirit of God is in my nostrils" (Job 27:3, KJV).

One of the major aspects of the Spirit's activity was His part in inspiring the writers who gave us the history, laws, promises, precepts, and prophecies of the Old Testament. The authors, who came from various walks of life, recognized themselves as instruments of the Divine Spirit.

In the Old Testament we read that the Holy Spirit came upon certain men in a peculiar way for some specific service which they were to render to God. They were especially equipped by the Spirit for the physical, mental, or spiritual activity committed to them by God. The Holy Spirit granted special wisdom to men like Moses and Joshua and David, to enable them to govern their people more righteously. At times He came upon the judges and leaders of Israel to equip them with unusual courage and physical strength for special emergencies or crises. By the Spirit, Gideon was prepared to do battle against the Midianites (Judges 6:34) and Samson was enabled to slay a lion (Judges 14:6). Then again, at the time of the building of the Tabernacle and the Temple as places for God's presence and man's worship, the Holy Spirit imparted special intellectual ability and artistic skills to men like Bezaleel and David, who were appointed to these tasks (see Exodus 31:1-5 and I Chronicles 28:11-12).

In the Old Testament there are also certain precious promises regarding the greater and more widespread ministry of the Holy Spirit that was yet to come. In Ezekiel there was the promise of the work of the Spirit in regeneration or the new birth:

> *A new heart also will I give you, and a new spirit will I put within you: and I will take away the stony heart out of your flesh, and I will give you an heart of flesh. And I will put my spirit within you, and cause you to walk in my statutes, and ye shall keep my judgments, and do them* (Ezek. 36:26-27, KJV).

Then, through the prophet Joel, God gave the wonderful promise of the fullness of the Holy Spirit, which was fulfilled on the Day of Pentecost:

> *And it shall come to pass afterward, that I will pour out my spirit upon all flesh; and your sons and your daughters shall prophesy, your old men shall dream dreams, your young men shall see visions: and also upon the servants and upon the handmaids in those days will I pour out my spirit* (Joel 2:28-29, KJV).

The Gospels are largely transitional between the Old Testament dispensation and the New Testament era. They are on the other side of Pentecost. However, they provide us with a rich treasury concerning the Holy Spirit's activity, especially in the life and ministry of our Lord Jesus Christ.

The conception of Christ's human nature in the womb of Mary was due to the operation of the Holy Spirit (Matt. 1:20). At the very beginning of His earthly ministry Christ was baptized by the Spirit and anointed for service (John 1:33). He was "led by the Spirit" into the wilderness for His conflict with Satan and returned victorious "in the power of the Spirit" (Luke 4:1, 14). All His mighty works were accomplished in the Spirit's power (Luke 4:18-19). He was raised from the dead by the agency of the Spirit (Rom. 8:1).

During His public ministry Jesus made several references to the Holy Spirit. To the Pharisees, He gave a warning concerning the sin against the Holy Spirit (Matt. 12:22-32). This was the sin of asserting that Christ's miracles were performed through the agency of a demon or evil spirit rather than through the power of the Holy Spirit. To Nicodemus, a member of the Sanhedrin, Jesus spoke about the necessity of being "born of the Spirit" in order to enter the kingdom of Heaven (John 3:1-7). In the synagogue at Capernaum, He declared that the Holy Spirit is the Source of spiritual life (John 6:63). To His disciples He said that the Heavenly Father gives "the Holy Spirit to those who ask him" (Luke 11:13). On the last day of the Feast of Tabernacles in Jerusalem, Jesus announced that, when the Holy Spirit came in His fullness, He would flow like rivers of living water out of the life of the believer (John 7:37-39).

Jesus had much to say about the person and ministry of the Holy Spirit when He met with His disciples for the last time in the Upper Room. He said to them:

> *It is to your advantage that I go away, for if I do not go away, the Counselor will not come to you; but if I go, I will send him to you. And when he comes, he will convince the world of sin and of righteousness and of judgment* (John 16:7-8).

Jesus told His disciples that the Holy Spirit would teach them all things and bring to their remembrance all that He had said to them (John 14:26). The Spirit would guide them into all the truth and show them things that were to come (John 16:13). The Spirit would dwell in them and abide with them forever (John 14:16-17). In addition, the Spirit would bear witness to Christ and glorify Him at all times (John 15:26; 16:14).

After the Resurrection, Jesus continued to speak to His disciples about the Holy Spirit. When He first appeared to them, He breathed on them and said: "Receive the Holy Spirit" (John 20:22). Later He commanded them to remain in Jerusalem until they were endued with the power of the Holy Spirit (Luke 24:49). He promised them that they would be baptized with the Holy Spirit within a few days and that they would receive power to become effective witnesses for Him throughout the world (Acts 1:5, 8).

When we come to The Acts of the Apostles we find ourselves on this side of Pentecost, in a new era. The Holy Spirit is everywhere in the foreground. He is the chief Personality in the Early Church. If the Father was the primary One of Old Testament revelation, and the Son was the primary One of the period covered by the Gospels, then certainly the Holy Spirit is the primary One since Pentecost. The Book of Acts is really the Acts of the Holy Spirit. He is the One who carries on the work of the Kingdom through the chosen instruments He calls and prepares for service. He is mentioned 49 times in the Book of Acts, all the way from the beginning (1:2) to the end (28:25).

On the Day of Pentecost the disciples were all "filled with the Holy Spirit" and from then on were called men and women "full of the Holy Spirit." Pentecost ushered in the dispensation of the Holy Spirit and began a new and more intimate relationship between the divine Spirit and the human personality. In the old dispensation, the Holy Spirit was granted to a *select few;* in the new dispensation He is available to *all.* In the old dispensation the Holy Spirit was given in a *limited way;* in the new, He is given *without measure*—in His fullness. Formerly the Spirit was imparted *periodically,* at certain times, for certain tasks; now He comes to abide *permanently* and empowers the believer for everyday living. Previously the emphasis was often on *physical prowess;* now the emphasis is on *inner purity* and *spiritual power.* Formerly the Holy Spirit came *upon* individuals; now He comes to dwell *in* us.

Why is it that the Holy Spirit could not be given in His fullness before the Day of Pentecost? The Apostle John gives us the answer to this question in his Gospel:

> *On the last day of the feast, the great day, Jesus stood up and proclaimed, "If any man thirst, let him come and drink. He who believes in me, as the scripture has said, 'Out of his heart shall flow rivers of living water.' " Now this he said about the Spirit, which those who believed in him were to receive, for as yet the Spirit had not been given, because Jesus was not yet glorified* (John 7:37-39).

Here is the answer. "As yet the Spirit had not been given, *because Jesus was not yet glorified."* The pattern of power had to be fixed before that power could be given. Jesus had to live, die, and rise again. Then the pattern was fixed. It is a Christlike power. God could now give with both hands.

In the Old Testament we read that the Spirit came upon Samson and he went out and slew a thousand Philistines (Judges 15:14-17). In the New Testament we don't read that the Holy Spirit came upon the disciples in the Upper Room, after which they went out and slew a thousand who were responsible for the crucifixion of Jesus.

Jesus gives us the pattern of the Holy Spirit, both in power and in purity. He was infinite sanctity and infinite sanity. He put proper content into the concept of the Holy

Spirit. Just as we cannot know what God is like apart from Jesus, so we cannot really understand what the Holy Spirit is like apart from Jesus. Now we know that the Holy Spirit is like Jesus. He too is infinite sanctity and infinite sanity. So we're no longer afraid of Him. To be filled with the Holy Spirit means that we become like Jesus.

The minister of a large church on the west coast said to Dr. E. Stanley Jones: "Every time you mention the Holy Spirit, cold chills go up and down my spine." When asked for the reason he explained, "I'm afraid of rampant emotionalism."

Dr. Jones replied: "My friend, you are patterning the Holy Spirit after certain people who have gone off into extremes. Christ is our Pattern. He was more filled with the Holy Spirit than anyone who ever walked the face of this earth. Are you afraid to be like Christ?"

"Ah, that makes a difference," exclaimed the preacher. "In that case there is no reason to be afraid." From resistance to receptivity within a few minutes! When he got his pattern straight, his attitude was correct.

It took the life, ministry, death, and resurrection of Jesus to give us the proper concept of the Holy Spirit.

In addition, it took the completed ministry of Christ to enable the Holy Spirit to minister to the needs of men in an unlimited manner. It is the special task of the Spirit to witness to the person of Christ, and He could not do this until that divine Person had stepped into the stream of human history and lived out a perfect and victorious life among men. It is the ministry of the Spirit to make redemption personal to the individual, and He could not do this without the actual death and resurrection of the Saviour. It is the supreme objective of the Holy Spirit to glorify Christ upon earth, but this was not possible until Jesus had ascended to the Father and been glorified in heaven. When the Holy Spirit came in power on the Day of Pentecost, it was a sign and seal that Jesus was now glorified and that He was the exalted Lord.

Pentecost, therefore, is significant from the standpoint of the acceptance of the completed work of Christ on the Cross. Salvation can now become the experience of all who accept the offer extended to them from the exalted Lord. The messengers of the Cross can proclaim freely the good news—even the forgiveness of sins and the gift of the Holy Spirit. Believers have in heaven their Saviour and His accepted work; while on earth, they have, even within themselves, the Holy Spirit, who applies the finished work of Christ and all its benefits to believers.

Pentecost was the beginning of a whole new era in the history of redemption and in God's dealings with man. And when Pentecost becomes personal to us, it can usher in a new day in our spiritual lives.

3

He Didn't Qualify

In the eighth chapter of the Book of Acts we read of a remarkable evangelistic movement that took place in the city of Samaria under the leadership of the lay evangelist, Philip. When Philip arrived in the city, he discovered that the residents were under the strange spell of a magician named Simon. The whole town was at his feet. He claimed to possess a certain supernatural power, which the people were led to believe was the power of God. Undoubtedly he was a clever charlatan who knew how to mislead the people by exploiting them for selfish ends, under the guise of religion.

Philip was a man filled with the Holy Spirit. Boldly he began to proclaim Jesus and the kingdom of God. Under the power of the Spirit he also performed many remarkable miracles. The Samaritans gave heed to Philip, listening to his message and observing his deeds, and before long they received the Christ whom he preached. They turned from the spurious to the real, from the magic of sorcery to the miracle of salvation. Their lives were transformed, their bodies healed. They were baptized in the name of Christ, and the city was filled with joy.

All this was disconcerting for Simon Magus. He lost his crowd and his money. He felt that Philip had taken away his following. Really, it was not Philip, but his Christ, who had won the hearts of the people. So, in keeping with the popular slogan, "If you can't lick 'em, join 'em," Simon decided to link up with Philip and thus reestablish himself in the favor of the people. He received baptism and posed as a believer.

When word reached the apostles in Jerusalem that Samaria had received the message of Christ, they sent Peter and John, who gave themselves especially to a ministry in behalf of the new converts. They emphasized the baptism with the Holy Spirit, and before long the people of Samaria received their personal Pentecost.

Simon Magus watched with keen interest. He had supposed that water baptism would initiate him. But no, now it seemed to be in the laying on of hands. He thought he too could obtain that powerful touch, so he sought after it. He brought money and offered it to the apostles, saying, "Give me also this power, that any one on whom I lay my hands may receive the Holy Spirit." With this world's goods he thought he could buy Heaven's power.

Simon Peter was probably suspicious of Simon Magus all along, but now he could see through him clearly. What a withering rebuke Peter gave him! "You want this power?" he thundered. "You want to bribe me? Your money perish with you. Your heart is not right in the sight of God and you have no part in this matter of the Holy Spirit. Repent and ask God to forgive you."

Simon Magus is a warning to all of us. He is a striking example of spiritual shallowness right in the church. He had been baptized and had been given his place in the fellowship of the community. He even posed as a leader. Yet he remained absurdly ignorant of the most elementary matters of the Christian life.

Like many in our churches today, Simon Magus had a very superficial conception of the Holy Spirit. In the first place, he thought of the Spirit as an intangible something— an *it*. Perhaps an influence, like "the spirit of '76" or "the school spirit." Or merely a driving force, like gasoline in the tank or electricity in the dynamo. He failed to understand that the Holy Spirit is a Person—One with whom we can have an intimate relationship.

As a Person, the Holy Spirit possesses all the attributes of personality. He has a mind, will, and affections. He thinks, He wills, and He feels. He performs personal acts: He speaks, testifies, calls, searches, and commands. Personal offenses may be committed against Him. He may be resisted, grieved, or sinned against. Thus the Holy Spirit should always be referred to with the personal pronoun "He."

The Holy Spirit is a divine Person. He is a Member of the Holy Trinity. He is God. He possesses all the attributes of divinity. He is omnipotent, omniscient, omnipresent, sovereign, and holy. Divine works are ascribed to Him—creation, preservation, regeneration, sanctification, and resurrection. As God, the Holy Spirit is the object of our honor and worship.

The Holy Spirit is the divine Executive of the Godhead. He is the Father and the Son in the world of men and in the hearts of men. He operates in nature and in history to carry out the decrees and works of the Godhead.

In the second place, Simon Magus thought that men had the authority to grant the Holy Spirit. He watched Peter and John laying hands on people and the people receiving the Holy Spirit. So he asked for power to lay hands on people and dispense this divine power. But no man, however spiritual or important he may be, has authority to bestow the Spirit of God. Sometimes the preacher or evangelist may lay hands on a person symbolically to help quicken his faith, but he cannot transmit the Holy Spirit by himself. The testimony of John the Baptist makes it clear that only Christ himself can baptize with the Holy Spirit (Matt. 3:11; Mark 1:8; Luke 3:16; John 1:33).

Bishop James Thoburn, one of the illustrious pioneer

missionaries of the Methodist church in India, was once preaching on the baptism of the Holy Spirit in a camp meeting. As he came to the close of his message, he stepped from behind the pulpit and in a quiet voice said to the congregation: "I must acknowledge that even I as a bishop cannot administer this baptism. But I had an understanding with a Friend of mine before this service began. He is the only One who can administer this baptism. He assured me that He would be present so that if anybody would say, 'I want this baptism,' He would be here to administer it, to receive a full consecration, and to honor a sincere faith." The good bishop was right. No man, only Christ can grant the Holy Spirit—and He is ever available to do so.

Simon Magus thought the Gift of the Holy Spirit could be bought for a price. He actually brought money and laid it at the apostles' feet. Men may traffic for gain in the institutional forms of religion, but they can never traffic in the Holy Spirit. The baptism of the Holy Spirit, like all the blessings of God, is a *gift*. It cannot be purchased, or acquired, or earned by merit. As a gift, it can only be received. God gives the Holy Spirit to them that *ask* Him. "Ask, and you will receive." Some people say, "I have been *seeking* the Holy Spirit for years." The truth is, they haven't been *seeking;* they have been *resisting*. One need not seek; just ask and receive.

Simon Magus thought of the baptism of the Holy Spirit as an end in itself. He thought of Pentecost in terms of power to do the showy, the spectacular thing. He wanted to get back his lost prestige and following. He wanted to make an impression on the people. He was more concerned about his *conquests* than his *character;* more concerned about what he was going to *do* than what he was going to *be*. He wanted the Holy Spirit so that he could use the Spirit, not so that the Spirit could use him. He wanted to glorify *self*, not the *Saviour*. But the Holy Spirit is the self-effacing Spirit. He does not talk about himself; He talks only about Christ. He seeks only to glorify Christ. And He will not allow us to talk about ourselves or to put ourselves on exhibition. To desire the Holy Spirit involves the willingness to die to self and the desire to glorify Christ in all things. We must be willing for Him to use us.

Simon Magus thought of the Holy Spirit only in terms of power. But the *power* of God is not given apart from *purity*. Sir Galahad, in Tennyson's great poem, is quoted as saying, "My strength is as the strength of ten because my heart is pure." Power is the result of holiness of heart and Christlikeness in disposition. Many people want power, but not purity. But God will not grant His power to an unsurrendered, self-centered person. He gives His power only to the one who is willing to be cleansed. The Spirit is first of all the *Holy* Spirit—the One who purifies. Then He is the Empowerer.

The fact of the matter is, Simon Magus was not only mistaken in his conception of the Holy Spirit, but he failed to qualify as a genuine candidate for the baptism with the Spirit. It is quite clear from Peter's rebuke that Simon was an unregenerated person, out of fellowship with the Heavenly Father. He had not genuinely repented of his sins and received God's gift of forgiveness. He had never truly been converted. And the baptism with the Holy Spirit is offered only to those who have been born of the Spirit.

But, someone argues, does not the record tell us that "even Simon himself believed" (Acts 8:13)? Yes, but we need to examine Simon's faith. A person can actually be a believer of a certain kind and yet not be saved.

John, in his Gospel, tells about many who "believed" in Christ during our Lord's public ministry:

> Now when he was in Jerusalem at the Passover feast, many believed in his name when they saw the signs which he did; but Jesus did not trust himself to them,

> *because he knew all men and needed no one to bear witness of man; for he himself knew what was in man* (John 2:23-25).

It is clear from this statement that there are some who are genuine believers and some who are not. There are some who have been attracted by certain things in the ministry of Christ and have yielded to Him a certain superficial allegiance. But the Master knows their inmost hearts and does not respond to them. Faith is more than giving mental assent to the truth. Genuine faith results in action. James writes in his Epistle: "Faith without works is dead . . . the devils also believe, and tremble" (2:20, 19, KJV).

Last year my wife and I made a trip through the islands of the South Pacific. Months ahead of time we made all the necessary arrangements and received complete information about the tour. We knew the number of each flight, the exact time of departure and arrival, the type of equipment, the cost of the ticket, the name of each airline, etc. We believed every word of the information and believed that the carriers would take us safely to our destination and back home again. But we could have believed all that and merely sat down and grown grey-headed, without ever crossing the Pacific. We had to act on our belief. We paid for our tickets and boarded the plane, bag and baggage. Up until the moment we walked up the steps, it was mere *belief*. The moment we stepped on board and fastened our seat belts, it became *trust*. We didn't actually say it in words, but in effect we said: "Captain, here we are for cloudy weather or for fair, for smooth flying or for rough. We commit ourselves to you and your crew, whose skill is a pledge that in five hours we shall be in Honolulu."

Or, to change the illustration, we may sincerely believe that if we write and mail a letter it will be delivered at its intended destination. But the belief does not become faith until we drop the letter into the mailbox and commit it to the postal authorities for their safe handling.

It is an absurd analogy, but we can believe every word in the Bible and yet be eternally lost. We have to act out our belief. Faith is essentially an act of the will—entrusting ourselves to the person of Christ. We believe that the Bible is God's Word, that Jesus died to save sinners, that He can forgive sin—certainly. But there comes that moment when our faith looks up to Him and we say in our hearts: "Lord Jesus, I believe You died for *me*. I believe You forgive me *now*. And I entrust my whole life into Your keeping, in sickness and in health, in adversity and in prosperity, in sorrow and in joy. I believe You can take me safely through the voyage of life to the other shore." That is faith!

Simon Magus exhibited a type of mental belief, but he did not exercise saving faith. And because his faith was superficial, his "conversion" was superficial. He was baptized and joined the company of believers, but his heart was not right with God. Peter made that clear. Simon joined the church, but not Christ. He kept fellowship with Philip, the evangelist, but was not in fellowship with the Saviour whom Philip preached. He gave up his sorcery, but did not surrender himself. He was still self-centered. He was absolutely ignorant of the basic principles of the Christian life. As a result, there was no real change in his life. He was still the same old Simon Magus.

This is the test of conversion. Did something happen in your life? Oh, I don't mean a great burst of emotion, a flash of lightning, or a sudden vision. But was there a real change in your life? Were the springs of your character transformed? Did you come into touch with the living Christ?

The manager of a store saw a young lad pounding the candy-vending machine with his fist, big tears streaming down his face. "What's the trouble, Son?" asked the manager. With choking voice the boy replied, "I put my money in the machine, but nothing happened!"

That's the trouble. A lot of people profess to believe, but nothing happens.

Conversion is not just an outer *change of label,* but an inner *change of life.* It is not merely horizontal, a change of position along the same plane, a moving out of one camp into another. Conversion is basically *vertical,* a change from one level of living to another, a stepping out of self into Christ.

Some years ago a Catholic priest in India had a Muslim cook working in his home. One day, very unexpectedly, the cook said to his master, "Sir, I want to become a Christian. Please baptize me." Without enquiring into his motives, the priest baptized the cook and received him into the church. As he poured the water over his head, the priest declared: "You are no longer Abdul [a Muslim name]; from now on you are Da-ood [David]." When the baptismal ceremony was over, the priest said to the new convert, "There is just one stipulation I have to make. On Friday you should not eat mutton, but only fish." (Muslims are expecially fond of mutton curry.)

For several weeks everything went well, until one Friday some very close friends of the cook appeared on the scene, and he felt he had to treat them with a feast of mutton curry. As he was preparing the meal, the aroma of the mutton came to the attention of the priest. He called the cook and said to him sternly, "Da-ood, I distinctly told you not to prepare mutton on Friday, only fish."

Da-ood replied, "Sir, this is not mutton; this is fish."

"You can't fool me," answered the priest. "I know you are preparing mutton."

And so they had an argument back and forth, the cook insisting the meat was fish, and the priest insisting it was mutton. Finally, in desperation, Da-ood said to his employer, "Sir, I'm just as clever as you are. You poured some water on my head and said, 'You are no longer Abdul; from now on you are Da-ood.' Well, I poured some water on this meat and said, 'You are no longer mutton; you are fish!'"

That is an example of a superficial type of conversion which ends in a mere change of label with no corresponding change in life. But in another city in India, a Hindu university student carefully studied the New Testament, came to the conclusion that Jesus is the Saviour of the world, and put his trust in Him. He was baptized and received into the church. Shortly afterward a Hindu friend of his stopped him on the street and said, "Prabhudas, I hear that you have changed your religion," Quick as a flash the new Christian answered, "No, you've got it all wrong. My religion has changed me!"

That is conversion. A genuine transformation of life!

What a difference there was between Simon, the magician, and Simon Peter, the apostle. Simon Magus "believed," but nothing happened; he was the same old person. Simon Peter also believed, but he was changed. When he first stood before Jesus, the Master looked at him and said: "You are Simon the son of John? You shall be called Cephas," or Peter, which means "rock" (John 1:42). When on one occasion Jesus said to His disciples, "Rejoice that your names are written in heaven, Peter's name was included in the list. Peter was also included in the final prayer of Jesus, when He said concerning His disciples, "Father . . . they have kept thy word. . . . they have believed that thou didst send me. . . . they are thine . . . I am glorified in them. . . . they are not of the world, even as I am not of the world" (John 17:1-19).

Peter was a candidate for the baptism with the Holy Spirit on the Day of Pentecost because he was a converted man. It is true he denied his Lord on the night of the Crucifixion, but he immediately repented of his sin and returned to his Lord. As for Simon Magus, he was not a fit candidate for the fullness of the Spirit, for he had never truly been converted. He was not in relationship with the Heavenly Father. He lacked true repentance and faith.

Before a man can be baptized with the Spirit, he first must be born of the Spirit.

4

This Is Where We Start

A man named Nicodemus came to Jesus one night for a private interview. Many have speculated about why he came at night. Some have suggested that Jesus was a very busy Man and was constantly surrounded by crowds of people during the day. The only time that He could be approached in private would be in the quiet of the late evening hours. Some have commented that Nicodemus himself, being a member of the Jewish Sanhedrin, had many responsibilities during the day and thus could find time to visit Jesus only after "office hours." Others suspect that Nicodemus was afraid of public opinion and so slipped in to see the Master under cover of darkness. Whatever the real reason may have been, the midnight setting became the occasion for discourse on a high-noon subject. You will find it recorded in John 3:1-15.

Nicodemus began the interview by paying Jesus a high compliment. "Rabbi," he said, "we know that you are a teacher come from God; for no one can do these signs that you do, unless God is with him." He recognized that Jesus was not just a run-of-the-mill religious commentator like the rest of the scribes. He was Someone special who spoke and acted with authority.

The Master, however, sidestepped the compliment and

spoke straight to the spiritual need of the visitor. Jesus looked beyond the man's flashy exterior and peered deep into his heart. He said to Nicodemus, "Truly, truly, I say to you, unless one is born of water and the Spirit, he cannot enter the kingdom of God. . . . 'You must be born anew.' "

THE NECESSITY OF THE NEW BIRTH

Here we are face-to-face with the dire necessity of the new birth. In the first place, it was Jesus himself who spoke these words. Not some man—a bishop of professor of religion perhaps—but the Son of God, who knew the heart of man better than anyone else. Then again, He used the strongest language possible. He didn't say, "It would be a good thing for a man to be born of the Spirit," or, "I recommend that you be born again." He said, "You *must* be born anew. . . . Unless one is born anew, he cannot see the kingdom of God." "Must," "unless," "cannot"—these are compelling words. And almost every time, Jesus prefaced His statement with the phrase, "Truly, truly, I say to you." In the language of that day, this was equivalent to saying, "I am about to say something of prime importance. You had better sit up and take notice." Furthermore, Jesus emphasized the necessity of the new birth over and over again. In slightly different form He repeated the command three times (vv. 3, 5, 7). Could there be any doubt of the significance He placed upon the subject?

In the second place, we begin to understand the necessity of the new birth when we realize to whom Jesus spoke these words. Nicodemus wasn't an ordinary man—someone off the street. He was an important person in Jewish society. The Gospel writer tells us that he was a Pharisee, a member of one of the strictest religious groups of the day. The Pharisees prided themselves in their observance of the Law, right down to the last detail. They fasted regularly. They prayed often. They paid a tithe of their income. They followed the traditions of the elders. They built tombs for the prophets. They zealously sought to make proselytes (see Matthew 23).

Nicodemus was also a "ruler of the Jews," a member of the Sanhedrin. He was one of the 70 elders who governed the religious and social life of the people. This meant that he had authority and prestige. He was educated and, most likely, financially well-off. He was respected in the community. And yet to such a man of religion and rank Jesus said, "You must be born anew." This is what was so startling to him. To say this to the man possessed with an evil spirit wouldn't be surprising. If He had said this to the woman taken in adultery or to the thief on the cross, it would be expected. But Nicodemus was an outwardly moral, seemingly upright Pharisee. Wasn't Jesus going a little too far?

Not in the least. Jesus says to each and every one of us today, regardless of our religous background, our nationality, or moral achievements—"You must be born again. Unless you are born of water and the Spirit, you cannot enter the kingdom of God."

Jesus would say to the illiterate inhabitant of the remote jungle and to the sophisticated university professor, "You must be born again." He would say to the poor man in the ghetto and to the millionaire on Lakeshore Drive, "You must be born again." He would say to Asian, African, Mongolian, and European, "You must be born again." He would say to Buddhist, Muslim, Hindu, and nominal Christian, "You must be born again." He says the same thing to every man, everywhere. The new birth is a universal human necessity.

In India the rural preacher delights in telling the story of the rich merchant who was being rowed across the river by the village boatman. As they started across, the merchant began to relate how many schools he had attended and how many books he had read. "How far did you study in school?" he asked the boatman.

"Sir," answered the oarsman, "I've never been to school in my life. I can't even read or write."

"Too bad. You have lost one-fourth of your life," remarked the merchant. Then he began to relate how far he had traveled and all the great sights he had seen. "How much traveling have you done?" he asked the boatman.

"I have never set foot outside this county," came the embarrassed reply.

"You unfortunate man! You have missed half of your life," commented the merchant. Then he began to boast of his wealth—his fields and houses and bank account. "How much money have you put away in the bank during your lifetime?" he asked.

"Sir, I have no money in the bank. I live from hand to mouth."

"Poor man! You have lost three-fourths of your life," remarked the merchant.

Suddenly, in midstream, a strong gust of wind overturned the boat, throwing both men into the water. The boatman, with strong strokes, started swimming toward the shore.

"Help, help!" cried the merchant. "I'm drowning!"

"What?" called back the boatman. "With all your money and education and travel you never learned how to swim? I'm telling you straight. You are about to lose your *whole* life!"

The one thing the merchant needed at that moment—the ability to swim—he did not have. Everything else was of no avail. Likewise, the one basic spiritual requirement for all men is the new birth. If anyone misses this, he misses life itself. There is no substitute.

Nature of the New Birth

When Jesus said to Nicodemus, "You must be born anew," Nicodemus completely misunderstood the import of these words. His mind drifted toward the scene of a midwife in a dimly lit room. He thought of the new birth purely in physical terms. He asked the Master, "How can a man be born when is old? Can he enter a second time into his mother's womb and be born?"

Jesus replied, "Nicodemus, I'm talking about being born of the Spirit. 'That which is born of the flesh is flesh, and that which is born of the Spirit is spirit.'" He was emphasizing the basic biological principle that "like produces like." From the vegetable comes the vegetable. From the animal comes the animal. From man comes man. Likewise, from the Spirit comes the spiritual. Physical birth can produce only physical life. It takes a spiritual birth to initiate spiritual life. Man, therefore, requires two births. He has to be conceived by his parents in order to receive physical life and enter into this world. He must also be conceived by the Spirit of God to receive spiritual life and enter the kingdom of God. By being born of human parents he becomes their son. By being born of the Spirit he becomes a child of God.

Thus the birth that Jesus is talking about is not physical but spiritual. In essence Jesus was saying to Nicodemus, "You can be conceived in your mother's womb a hundred times—yes, a thousand times—but all you will have will be physical life. What you need is a spiritual birth wrought by the Spirit of God himself."

Man is the only creature who is capable of living in two distinct worlds at the same time. As a physical being, created in the spiritual image of God, he can live in both the physical and the spiritual realms. He can be both a son of man and a child of God. It is possible, however, for a person to be very much alive physically and at the same time to be spiritually dead. He may be a "walking corpse," moving about in the flesh, but dead in the spirit. Paul, in his Epistles, often describes the sinner as being "dead in trespasses and sins"

(KJV; Eph. 2:1, 5; Col. 3:13). He declares solemnly that "the wages of sin is death" (Rom. 6:23).

Why is it that many people have no desire to read God's Word or spend time in prayer? They're spiritually dead and do not know the One who inspired the Book. Why is it they have no love for the church and seem to get nothing out of the worship services? They're spiritually dead and are insensitive to the movements of the Spirit. Why is it they neither witness for Christ nor serve their fellowman? Because they're dead and insensitive to the spiritual needs of others.

I once heard of a black preacher who was pastor of a sophisticated, urban congregation. He preached and labored faithfully, but the people did not seem to respond. So, in despair, one Sunday morning he declared that the church was dead and announced that he would conduct its funeral on the following Sunday. "There's only one thing to do with a corpse," he said, "and that is to bury it."

On the appointed day, motivated by sheer curiosity, the people crowded the church to participate in the "funeral." The ushers rolled in a casket, and the pastor preached the funeral sermon. At the close he announced that the casket would now be opened and anyone who so desired could come forward and review the remains of the dead church. When the first person leaned over and looked into the casket, he jumped back with a surprised look on his face. So did the next, and next. For on the bottom of the casket the preacher had placed a large mirror, so that everyone who peered in saw his own reflection!

It is a sad fact that many churches today are spiritually dead, and they're dead because the people who make up the congregation are dead. They have never been born of the Spirit and quickened with spiritual life. The tragedy is that often they do not realize they're dead, and they'll never know the truth about themselves until they gaze into the mirror of God's Word.

When a man is born of the Spirit, he suddenly comes alive. His conscience is alive to the promptings of the Spirit. His mind is alive to spiritual truth. Prayer takes on new meaning as dialogue with a Friend. God's Word becomes a personal love letter. Witness and service become a spontaneous expression of love.

Furthermore, when a man is born of the Spirit, he receives a new nature. As a child of God, he partakes of the holiness of God. This results in a radical change of character and conduct. The Apostle Paul described it thus: "If any one is in Christ, he is a new creation; the old has passed away, behold, the new has come" (II Cor. 5:17). This is more than just patchwork or an outer reformation. It is an inner, moral transformation. Like the young man who testified at the close of a summer "Ashram" (retreat): "I came here expecting the Lord to do some repair work, but instead He has given me a brand-new engine!"

A few years ago a Methodist minister in a midwestern city preached a sermon on the new birth at the regular Sunday morning service. He used the catchy title "New Tricks for Old Dogs." Several days later an attractive young lady called on him in the church office. "Do you remember the sermon you preached on the new birth?" she asked. "Well, that message really got through to me." Then she went on to relate how she had been having an affair with a well-to-do businessman in town. Whenever he made a business trip out of town, she accompanied him on the plane and stayed with him in his hotel room. The man's wife had become aware of the situation and was brokenhearted.

As a result of the minister's sermon, the young lady became convicted of her sin, went home from the service, prayed in desperation, and surrendered her life to Christ. When she arose from her knees, she immediately called the wife on the phone, asked for forgiveness, and assured her that she would break off the relationship with her husband.

The next day she called on the businessman in his office. "It's all off," she said. "This is the last time you will see me."

"You will be short of cash, Honey," he said. "You won't be able to buy all those beautiful clothes anymore."

"That's alright," she replied. "I'll find a job and support myself."

"You'll miss all the travel and good times," he continued.

"I have found a new joy in life," she replied softly.

"What's wrong with you?" he asked angrily. "Have you fallen in love with someone else?"

For a moment the young lady was taken aback. Then she smiled and said, "Yes, that's it. I have fallen in love with Someone else."

He stood up, pale with rage. "Tell me his name and I'll kill him," he shouted, pounding his desk with his fist.

"I'm afraid you can't do that," came the quiet reply. "You see, I have just fallen in love with Jesus!"

As the young lady finished her story, she said to the minister, "You see, Pastor, something happened inside of me that Sunday morning. I'm not the same person. It's as if I had been born all over again."

THE MYSTERY OF THE NEW BIRTH

Seeing the puzzled look on the face of His visitor, Jesus went on to say, "[Nicodemus,] do not marvel that I said to you, 'You must be born anew.' The wind blows where it wills, and you hear the sound of it, but you do not know whence it comes or whither it goes; so it is with every one who is born of the Spirit" (vv. 7-8).

In other words, there is a mystery about the birth of the Spirit. The new birth is something difficult to explain or understand. But one does not need to stumble over the mystery. It is not necessary to understand all about the new birth before a person can experience its results in his life. It is like the wind, says Jesus. We don't know all about the wind, where it comes from and where it goes; but we see its effects everywhere. We feel its cool breeze on our faces. We see it scatter the leaves all over the yard. We watch it bend the limbs of the trees. So it is with the Spirit of God. We cannot see Him or understand all about Him. But we know when He breathes new life into us. We joyfully respond as He witnesses to us that we are now the children of God. We see the change that He effects in our daily lives.

There are many mysteries in life. Electricity is one of them. How much does the average person really understand about electricity? But is it necessary for us to know all about electricity before we can enjoy its benefits? All we need to know is how to flip the switch, and immediately we can enjoy the light or turn on the motor.

The food we eat is a mystery. Do we fully understand how meat and vegetables and fruit turn into blood and bone, cell and tissue? But this doesn't keep us from going to the table three times a day. All we know is that when we eat we receive new life and energy. I don't understand how a brown cow eats green grass and gives white milk. But that doesn't stop me from drinking milk.

There are those who hesitate to accept the truth of the new birth because they find it difficult to understand or explain. But they do not need to fully understand all about it in order to experience it. In fact, after they have been born of the Spirit and the eyes of their understanding have been opened to spiritual things, they will understand far more about the new birth than they were able to do previously. A few months of walking in the Spirit will teach them more than a dozen courses on the subject.

The new birth is a mystery because it is a miracle—a miracle wrought by the Spirit of God himself. It is, therefore, in the realm of the supernatural.

There are three stark miracles in the world. The first is the miracle of creation, when God said, "Let there be," and there was. This was the introduction of life into dead matter. The second was the miracle of the Incarnation, when God took on the form of man so that through Christ He might reconcile the world unto himself. This was the invasion of the life of God into human history. The third is the miracle of the new creation, when a person is born of the Spirit. This is the introduction of God's life into the life of an individual. Something new is begun.

Many beautiful gospel songs have been written to describe the miracle of the new birth. Here are two by John W. Peterson:

It took a miracle to put the stars in place;
It took a miracle to hang the world in space;
But when He saved my soul, cleansed and made me
whole,
It took a miracle of love and grace!

I believe in miracles;
I've seen a soul set free.
Miraculous the change in one
Redeemed on Calvary.
I've seen the lily lift its head
Up through the stubborn sod;
I believe in miracles,
For I believe in God.

THE MEANS OF THE NEW BIRTH

After Jesus had emphasized the necessity of the new birth and had sought to describe its nature and results, Nicodemus turned to Jesus and asked pointedly, "How can this be?" In reply Jesus said, "No one has ascended into heaven but he who descended from heaven, the Son of man. And as Moses lifted up the serpent in the wilderness, so must the Son of man be lifted up, that whoever believes in him may have eternal life" (vv. 13-14).

Thus Jesus made it clear that the new birth is made possible by His vicarious death on the Cross. There was no other way. He gave His life that we might have life. He died that we might live. The Son of God became the Son of Man, that the sons of men might become the sons of God.

The story is told of two brothers who lived in the same town. The elder brother was the local judge and was an upright, good man, respected by all. The younger brother, however, was a wayward young man, always getting into trouble. He refused to accept the advice of his elder brother; and furthermore, since his brother was the judge in the city, he felt he would never be condemned for any crime he committed.

One day the younger brother became involved in a drinking brawl, struck another man, and killed him. He was arrested and brought to trial. His own brother was the judge. The jury rendered a verdict of "guilty of murder," and the judge decreed that the criminal should be hung. When the young man heard the decree, he rushed up to the front, fell at the feet of the judge, and cried out, "You are my brother! Have you no love for me? Are you condemning me to die?"

The judge replied solemnly, "It is true I am your brother, but this is a court of law and here I sit as your judge. You have committed murder. You must die for your crime."

The young man was escorted away and placed in solitary confinement. As the time for his execution drew near, he became more despondent and fearful. Just an hour or two before he was to be hung, the elder brother, dressed in his official robe, came to the prison and asked for the privilege of seeing the prisoner. When he stepped into the cell, he said, "There in the court of law, I was the judge and had to see that justice prevailed. But here I stand as your brother who loves you and wants to set you free. But there is only one way. Take off your prison clothes and put on my judge's robe, and walk out of here a free man. I will take your place."

The two men exchanged clothing, and the younger brother walked out into freedom. Not long after, the prison guards came, took the prisoner out, and hung him. Suddenly the younger brother came running from a distance, threw his arms around the lifeless form of his brother, and wept bitterly. "O my brother," he cried, "you died in my place!"

The guards were astonished when they realized what had happened. But it was too late. A life had been given. The penalty was paid.

This is exactly what Christ has done for us. We all stood before the Judge of the universe, guilty and condemned. The verdict read, "The wages of sin is death." But because He loved us with an everlasting love, the Judge became our Elder Brother that He might become our Redeemer. "God was in Christ reconciling the world to himself." Christ took our sin upon himself and died in our place. He took the initiative and did for us what we could not do by ourselves.

The important question now is, What are we going to do about what God has done for us? He has acted. How shall we react? Shall we respond in gratitude or ingratitude? In faith or disbelief?

Faith is the door into life. Jesus said, "Whoever believes . . . may have eternal life." John wrote, "To all who received him [Christ], who believed in his name, he gave power to become children of God." We must accept the truth that Christ died for our sins. We must receive the gift that He offers us in a nail-pierced hand. We must put our trust in Him and commit ourselves into His keeping.

When we respond in faith—which also is a gift from God—then the Holy Spirit becomes the Agent of regeneration in our lives. It is He who quickens us from death unto life. As the Divine Obstetrician, He "delivers" us into the new world of God's kingdom and breathes into us the very life of God. We are then "born of the Spirit" and become "children of God."

Jesus says to every man, "You must be born anew. Unless a man is born of water and of the Spirit, he cannot enter into the kingdom of God." This is the *sine qua non*, the indispensable requisite for spiritual life. The Christian walk begins with the birth of the Spirit.

The new birth is the prerequisite for the baptism with the Spirit. The gift of the fullness of the Spirit is offered, not to sinners, but to the children of God. It was to His immediate disciples—men who had forsaken all to follow Him, men who had been converted and whose names were written in the book of life—that Jesus promised they would be baptized with the Spirit "before many days."

But once a man is born of the Spirit, he is a candidate for the baptism with the Spirit. This is God's intention and will. This is Christ's provision and promise. No child of God should be satisfied until he has claimed his full inheritance in Christ and experienced a personal Pentecost in his own life. To fail to do so is to fall short of God's highest will and to miss His finest gift.

5

What Happened Upstairs?

Many things took place on that eventful day in an Upper Room in Jerusalem. But the danger for us is to see only the outward physical manifestations and miss the real inward transformation that resulted. There was the sound like a rushing mighty wind that filled the whole house where the disciples were assembled. There were cloven tongues like fire that rested upon each of them. The disciples all spoke in other languages so that people of all nations gathered in Jerusalem could understand in their own native tongues what was being said.

But is this what we should expect from Pentecost today —wind, fire, other languages? Or is there something deeper involved?

We must distinguish between the *passing* and the *permanent* aspects of Pentecost; between the *temporary* and the *timeless;* between the *incidental* and the *funda-*

mental; between the *historical framework* and the *personal fact.*

The Temporary Framework	The Permanent Fact
1. The Day of Pentecost, a Jewish agricultural festival commemorating the first-fruits of the harvest	1. Any day that we are willing to meet the conditions; a spiritual festival representing the fruit of the Spirit
2. One hundred twenty disciples in an Upper Room in Jerusalem	2. Any number of disciples anywhere, united, yielded, and praying for the outpouring of the Spirit
3. Cloven tongues like fire	3. The refining fire of the Holy Spirit, sanctifying the individual and empowering him for service
4. Extraordinary speaking in different languages	4. The demonstration that in the Church of the living Christ there is neither Jew nor Gentile, bond nor free, and that the gift of the Holy Spirit is for *all.*
5. Outer signs and wonders	5. Inner strength and well-being of holiness. The greatest sign of all and the greatest wonder—adequate power for holy living and for fruitful service

Thus we must distinguish between the picture and the frame, between the gift and the wrappings. On the one hand, the *Day of Pentecost,* as a great historical drama in God's plan of salvation, is an event of the past and cannot be repeated. It was the beginning of a new era and the birthday of the Church, and in its historical significance can never be repeated any more than the Manger, or Calvary, or the Resurrection, or the Ascension can be repeated. On the other hand, the *experience of Pentecost* has been repeated over and over again down through the Christian centuries and can be repeated—anytime, anywhere a disciple or group of disciples is willing to meet the conditions of obedience, surrender, and faith.

Many times in the Book of Acts other people were filled with the Spirit. Thousands of Christians across the world can testify today to a personal experience of Pentecost. Paul, in his Epistles, plainly commands that all Christians be filled with the Spirit; and Peter, on the Day of Pentecost, explicitly stated that the gift of the Holy Spirit is for all. "The promise is unto you, and to your children, and to all that are afar off, even as many as the Lord our God shall call" (Acts 2:39, KJV).

A careful reading of the Acts of the Apostles reveals to us that the fundamental results of the experience of Pentecost are three: (1) The plentitude of the Spirit, (2) purity of heart, and (3) power for service.

The Plentitude of the Spirit

Luke, the historian, tells us that on the Day of Pentecost the 120 disciples were all *filled with the Holy Spirit*. This was basic to everything else that followed.

As has already been pointed out, it does not mean that this was the first time the Holy Spirit was operating in the lives of Christ's followers. The Holy Spirit was not a stranger to them. Jesus made this very clear in His last discourse in the Upper Room, when He met with His disciples for the celebration of the Passover. He said, "You know him [the Holy Spirit], for he dwells with you" (John 14:17). At the same time Jesus made it clear that the disciples would shortly enter into a more intimate relationship with the Holy Spirit. "He dwells with you, and *will be in you* . . . with you for ever. . . . Before many days you shall be baptized with the Holy Spirit" (John 14:17, 16; Acts 1:5). In other words, this was to be the *fullness* of the Spirit.

Here again we must be careful to understand what this means. We must not get the idea that the Holy Spirit is fragmented or disconnected, and that He comes only in parts or portions, so that when we are born of the Spirit we receive part of Him, and then when we are baptized with the Spirit we receive the rest of Him. The Holy Spirit is a Person, a perfect Personality. He cannot be split up into segments. He cannot be divided into "more" or "less" stages. It may be possible for us to be split personalities, to be double-minded, but not for Him. When we are converted, we *have* the Holy Spirit—*all* of the Holy Spirit that we will ever have. So to be baptized or filled with Spirit certainly does *not* mean that we get *more* of the Spirit; rather, the Holy Spirit gets *more of us.* For though we have all of the Spirit, He does not have all of us. He must have uncontested control of our lives, so that He does not simply dwell in us, but dwells unhindered; that is, in all His fullness.

In a certain city the members of the ministerial association were making plans for a city-wide evangelistic campaign. Many persons were being suggested for the evangelist. When someone proposed that they invite Dwight L. Moody, one minister objected strongly. "We've had Moody before," he argued. "Why do you want to invite him again and again? Does Moody have a monopoly on the Holy Spirit?"

"No," replied another quietly, "but the Holy Spirit has a monopoly on Dwight L. Moody."

That's the secret of the Spirit-filled life. The Holy Spirit must have a monopoly on us.

But someone asks, "Cannot a person be regenerated and filled with the Spirit at the same time? Cannot a person make a complete consecration to Christ the first time he comes to Him? Cannot God perform both acts of regeneration and sanctification at one time?"

The answer is, theoretically, "Yes." There is no limitation on God's part. He will fulfill His promises the moment we meet the conditions. But from the practical standpoint, the records of the New Testament and the experiences of thousands of sincere Christians confirm the fact that, as a rule, one does not experience the birth of the Spirit and the baptism with the Spirit at one and the same time. The limitation is on our part.

Some time ago I read Lawson's little book, *Deeper Experiences of Famous Christians.* I found the theology and nomenclature varied considerably. Each individual expressed his experience within the particular theological framework and terminology of his own denomination. But the common denominators in all the experiences were apparent. This "deeper experience" was always subsequent to the experience of conversion, and usually followed a period of great soul-searching and spiritual desperation. There was a new and deeper surrendering of the individual self to God. There was a greater sense of the presence and power of God in the person's life, as he began living on a permanently higher plane.

There seems, therefore, to be general agreement that the infilling of the Holy Spirit comes after the crisis of conversion. The individual makes an initial surrender to Christ when he receives Him as Saviour. But then as he walks day by day in the Christian life, he begins to discover that there are areas of his life that are not fully committed to the Master's will. Christ is not really Lord in every part of his being. He also discovers that within himself are attitudes, desires, and reactions that are unchristian and act as a drag on his spiritual life. He now makes a fuller surrender of himself, crowns Jesus as King in his life, and permits the Holy Spirit to sanctify his innermost being. To this experience countless sincere Christians could testify.

Suppose you turn on the ceiling light in the living room of your home. Immediately light floods the room and dispels the darkness. But still there may be a few areas in the room where partial darkness prevails. The couch, the chairs, the piano, and other pieces of furniture cast shadows across the room. Underneath the couch it may be quite dark. Then suppose you remove all furniture from the room. What happens? The light immediately permeates every part of the room, for now there are no longer any hindrances. The amount of light is the same, but the area of penetration is greater.

In the same way, the Holy Spirit may be residing in a believer and yet may not be able to penetrate every part of his being. There are too many hindrances. Resentments, uncontrolled temper, pride, doubt, and other unchristian attitudes are casting shadows in his heart. What the individual needs is not more of the Spirit, but to allow the Spirit to possess more, yes, *all* of him. Then he will be "filled with the Spirit."

Purity of Heart

The second basic result of Pentecost was heart purity. Peter made this clear when he addressed the first Christian council at Jerusalem: "And God who knows the heart bore witness to them, giving them the Holy Spirit just as he did to us; and he made no distinction between us and them, but *cleansed their hearts* by faith" (Acts 15:8-9, italics mine).

In essence, what Peter said was this: "Exactly the same thing that God did in our hearts on the Day of Pentecost, He has now performed in the hearts of the Gentiles." And what was it God did? He "cleansed their hearts by faith."

The word "heart" is used symbolically to denote the seat of our affections, emotions, desires, attitudes, and motives. Cleansing of the heart, therefore, refers to a radical inner cleansing of the center of our personalities.

Such cleansing was very evident in the lives of Christ's disciples. Before Pentecost, on many occasions they manifested un-Christlike attitudes and reactions. For example, they exhibited pride. They argued among themselves who was greatest in the kingdom of Heaven (Luke 9:46). They manifested selfishness. They requested Jesus to grant them thrones on the right and on the left when He established His kingdom (Mark 10:35-40).

They also demonstrated narrow-mindedness. Once when they saw someone who was not of their group casting out demons, they sought to restrain him (Mark 9:38). The disciples at times reacted in anger. Once, while traveling through Samaria, when they were refused lodging and hospitality by the Samaritans, they wanted to call down fire upon these people (Luke 9:54-56). They exhibited carnal fear and cowardice. On the night of Christ's arrest and trial, they fled and hid themselves. Peter denied his Lord three times (Matt. 26:56, 69-75).

At Pentecost the Holy Spirit performed radical spiritual surgery in the disciples' hearts. Pride was replaced with humility, self-seeking with the spirit of service, narrow-mindedness with sympathy, anger with love, and carnal fear with holy boldness. Many present-day disciples of Christ need a similar divine operation in their lives.

The desire to be filled with the Spirit must be accompanied by the willingness to be made pure. The Spirit of God is fundamentally the *Holy* Spirit. It is a law in logic that when you affirm something you automatically deny the opposite. When you say of an object, "This is white," you are automatically saying, "It is not black." When you say, "This is a rectangle," you at the same time deny that it is a circle. When you declare, "This is wood," it means it is not metal. In the same way, the Holy Spirit is absolutely, irrevocably opposed to evil.

To affirm that I want to be filled with the Spirit is to declare that I am willing to be emptied of all my unholy attitudes and spirit. Many of us pray with our lips, "Lord, fill me," but inwardly we say, "Lord, don't expose my resentments; don't disturb my comforts." But God cannot compromise with sin. He puts His finger upon anything that gets between us and Him, and between us and our fellow-men. With the fire of the Holy Spirit, He wants to purify us in our innermost being.

An evangelist friend of mine was invited to conduct a preaching mission in a certain city and was entertained in the home of a middle-aged couple. When the hostess escorted the evangelist ot the guest room, she said in a welcome voice, "Now, I want you to make yourself completely at home. Hang your suits up in the closet and put your other clothes in the drawers. This is your room." The visitor took the hostess at her word, removed everything from his suitcase, and spread it out on the bed. But when he went to the closet to hang up his clothes, he found it jammed full of suits, dresses, slacks, and topcoats, with no empty hanger. When he opened the top drawer of the dresser, it was full of old clothing and rags. He tried the next; it was full also. Likewise, the bottom drawer was crammed with old picture albums and family heirlooms. There was absolutely no room for his clothes, so he put them all back into his suitcase.

When we say to the Holy Spirit, "Make yourself at home," we can't expect to keep anything hidden in the secret closets and drawers of our hearts. We must be willing to be emptied of all that is contrary to His nature and will. He must be more than a Guest; He must be Lord. This means He will do a thorough job of housecleaning and will rearrange the furniture to His own plan.

POWER FOR SERVICE

The third major result of Pentecost is power. Just before He ascended to the Father, Jesus said to His disciples, "You shall receive power when the Holy Spirit has come upon you; and you shall be my witnesses in Jerusalem and in all Judea and Samaria and to the end of the earth" (Acts 1:8). On previous occasions He had commanded them to tarry in

Jerusalem until they were "clothed with power from on high" (Luke 24:49; Acts 1:4).

Here again we notice the difference in the lives and ministry of the disciples before and after Pentecost. Before the outpouring of the Holy Spirit in His fullness, the disciples often displayed moments of weakness. Sometimes there was vacillation, or doubt, or a carnal fear of men. This was especially true in the last days before Calvary. They forsook their Master and went into hiding. Peter shamefully denied his Lord. But after the experience of Pentecost, the disciples displayed a stronger faith, a new spirit of confidence and courage. They possessed power beyond themselves to withstand persecution and temptation, and to witness boldly to the resurrection of the Lord.

How the Church today needs this supernatural power—power to reach out beyond the confines of brick and mortar, and to carry the spiritual offensive into the strongholds of society! The Church needs power to break out of routine and formality, and to perform exploits in the Master's name; power to call people to repentance and true righteousness; power to transform individuals and change society!

The Church of our day has great buildings, but little boldness. It has numbers, but little nerve. It has comfort, but no courage. It has status, but lacks spirit. It has prestige, but no power.

I remember watching the TV program "Candid Camera" a few years ago. A woman coasted downhill in a car and rolled into a filling station. "Fill it up with regular," she said to the smiling attendant, "and check the oil, please."

Imagine the look of astonishment on the man's face when he lifted up the hood and found there was no engine! The Church in many places reminds me of a car that has lost its engine. It has lost its source of power.

One New Year's Day, in the Tournament of Roses parade at Pasadena, Calif., a beautiful float came along

Colorado Avenue in the middle of the procession. Its collection and arrangement of flowers was breathtaking. Suddenly the truck which was powering the float sputtered and came to a standstill. It was out of gas. The whole parade was held up while someone went for a two-gallon can of gas. The crowd roared with laughter when somebody said, "That float represents the Standard Oil Company!" With all the resources of this great company at its disposal, its truck was out of gas!

The Church today need not go on in its powerless, ineffective condition. All the mighty resources of the Holy Spirit are at its disposal. The individual Christian need not remain spiritually weak and anemic. He can tarry in surrender and faith and be "clothed with power from on high." Just as atomic power represents the release of hidden forces in the physical world, so Pentecost represents the release of invisible forces in the realm of personality.

Again, let us understand clearly that power cannot be separated from purity. Power is not an entity in itself. It is basically the unhindered flow of the Spirit's energy in and through a life that is utterly yielded to Christ and has been subjected to radical surgery by His skillful hand. We cannot experience the power until we're willing to be made pure. Purity and power go hand in hand.

These then are the permanent and fundamental characteristics of Pentecost: (1) the fullness of the Holy Spirit; (2) purity of heart; and (3) power for witnessing and service. These are the results that took place in the lives of the apostles and early Christians in the first century, and these are the results that can take place in the lives of any and all of Christ's followers in the twentieth century.

Pentecost was not merely a historical event; it is a a present possibility. It was not a fleeting incident, external to the real core and course of the life of the Church. It is a profoundly vital experience with abiding values and permanent principles. It was not only a particular day, but is an extended dispensation. The baptism of the Holy Spirit was not for the Apostolic Church only; it rests, as both obligation and opportunity, upon the Church of every generation.

Pentecost is age-long and planet-wide. Given a child of God utterly yielding, trustfully expecting, any room may become an Upper Room, any day a Day of Pentecost.

6

What Must I Do?

Now having established that the experience of Pentecost is the birthright of all God's children, and having examined closely the permanent results of Pentecost, we come to the all-important question, How do we receive the fullness of the Holy Spirit?

There are some who declare that we simply grow into the experience. They say, "Just give me time. Let me grow. After a while I will be more like a saint." All this sounds good, but it ignores the facts both of Scripture and of general Christian experience. It is a false and dangerous idea. As A. W. Tozer reminds us, time has no more power to sanctify a person than space has. After all, time is only a human fiction. It is only our way of experiencing reality. It is change, not time, that leads us into the deeper life—change wrought by the Holy Spirit himself. The truth of the matter is, there are many who were much better Christians shortly after the time of their conversion than they are right now. Why? Because they have not sought to be filled with the Spirit, and as a result have settled down to a halfhearted, dilatory Christian life. They have been drifting—not growing.

Now there is a certain sense in which we do grow *toward* the experience of the fullness of the Holy Spirit—that is, there is often a process or series of minor crises that leads to the final event of the infilling. Most of us have to *grow up* to a certain place in our Christian lives where we are able to see the need of a deeper work of cleansing and are able to make a more complete surrender of ourselves to Christ. Perhaps we ought to say *grow down* rather than *grow up* to this place of readiness. For the truth of the matter is that not many of us grow gradually and steadily. We are too stubborn and self-centered for that.

God has to bring us *down,* again and again, with crisis after crisis. He has to let us get knocked down, to let us try and fail perhaps several times, until we finally are so utterly desperate that we come to the absolute end of all our own resources and strength. We discover that we are not just sinners, but sin itself, that in us "dwelleth no good thing." We realize that all our working and striving are as filthy rags, tainted with the subtle evil called self-glorification. Then in sheer desperation we give up, and make the surrender, and cast ourselves upon the grace of God. If we think that comes about by pleasant and gradual growth, we are sadly mistaken. It is really a facing of a series of crises, a seeking that is progressively more desperate, until finally we receive the fullness of the Spirit.

Surrender Your Self

The first step in the Spirit-filled life is self-surrender. It has already been pointed out that the reason why many Christians are not filled with the Spirit is because the Spirit does not have all of them. They have not fully surrendered themselves to the Saviour and crowned Him King in their lives.

Why does the Christian faith place so much emphasis on self-surrender? Simply because the unsurrendered self is the cause of all our spiritual problems. Just as the fingers are rooted in the hand, so our sins are rooted in the palm of the unsurrendered self. Why does a man steal? To gain something for the self. Why does a man lie? To protect the self. Why does a man get angry? The self has been crossed. Why does a man get jealous? Something is getting ahead of the self. Why does a man think evil thoughts? To gain pleasure for the self.

Take the little word SIN. Right in the middle of the word is the letter *I*. It is the unsurrendered ego, the I, that is the root of our problems.

The unsurrendered self is manifested in many different forms. Sometimes it manifests itself in *self-seeking*. The individual, instead of seeking first the kingdom of God and His righteousness, seeks his own pleasure, position, plans, and prestige. Like the prodigal son who said to his father, "Give me—give me." He wanted to take his possessions and spend them on his own interests. And like the two disciples, James and John, who requested Jesus to permit them to sit on His right and left when He established His kingdom on earth. They were seeking for thrones and scepters to glorify themselves, while Jesus was on His way to the Cross to give himself for the redemption of the world.

Sometimes the unsurrendered ego manifests itself in *self-love*. The individual, instead of loving God supremely and his neighbor as himself, is actually in love with himself. He thinks more highly of himself than he ought to think, and becomes proud and censorious. A university professor was so conceited and infatuated with himself that the students jokingly referred to him as "a self-made man who worshipped his creator."

The unsurrendered ego sometimes manifests itself in *self-assertion*. The individual likes to be the center of the group. He likes to dominate the conversation. He likes to talk about himself, where he has been, and what he has accomplished. He frequently makes use of the personal pronoun "I."

When my brother was working on his master's thesis at Hartford, Conn., some years ago, he rented a typewriter from a local agent. As the man was setting up the typewriter in the apartment, he made a few casual remarks about his business that proved most interesting. He said to my brother, "You know, the letter on the keyboard that we have to replace more often than any other is the letter *I*. The reason for this," he went on to explain, "is not so much because people use this letter more than any other, but when they use it, they strike the key so hard!"

At times the unsurrendered self is manifested by *self-indulgence*. The individual is motivated, not by principle, but by desire. This may lead to excess, gluttony, enslaving habits, or even immorality.

Self-justification is another characteristic of the unsurrendered ego. The person finds it difficult to admit that he was mistaken. He is slow to apologize. He constantly seeks to justify his actions and to vindicate his position.

Then there is *self-sufficiency*. The individual, instead of relying wholly on the resources and grace of God, depends on his own wisdom, his own ability, his own efforts. Like Peter, who on the night of Christ's arrest and trial boasted that, if all the other disciples forsook the Master and fled, he alone would be faithful to the end, even unto death. But when the time of testing came, he miserably failed and denied his Lord three times. He thought he was strong enough on his own.

A little girl was singing to herself in the living room of the house one day, while her mother was working in the kitchen. It was an old, familiar song, but this must have been the revised version. The mother smiled as she overheard the daughter singing, "Count your blessings, name them one by one, and it will surprise the Lord what you have done." Self-sufficiency!

Then again, the unsurrendered self is manifested by *self-will*. Perhaps this is the crux of the matter. The individual, instead of seeking God's will in every decision and area of life, often desires to go his own way. In his wonderful book entitled *The Great Divorce*, C. S. Lewis suggests that in the last analysis there are only two groups of people in the world. The first group comprises those who say to God, "Not my will, but Thine, be done." Jesus was the great Example of this attitude in life, when He prayed this very prayer in the Garden of Gethsemane, just before His crucifixion. The second group of people are those to whom God eventually has to say, "Not My will, but thine be done. You wanted to have your way; alright, you can have it—forever." And Lewis suggests that when God eventually and decisively says this to any man, that is hell.

The self is usually the last thing we are willing to surrender. It's easy to *give to* Christ, to give *things;* it's hard to *give up* to Christ, to present *ourselves.* We usually are willing to give anything to Christ—money, possessions, even service—everything but our own selves. I remember a layman in India who confessed before the congregation, "All these years I have given my offerings faithfully to the Lord, but I have never really given myself." A young single missionary, who went out to India to pastor an English-speaking congregation in a large city, said in a retreat one day, "I had left my home and loved ones, a good job and a fine salary, to come to India to work for God, but until today I had not really surrendered myself." Simon Peter, acting as spokesman for the disciples, said to the Master on one occasion, "Lo, we have left everything and followed you. What then shall we have?" (Matt. 19:27) Note the last part of the statement. Peter had given up his home, his boats, and his fishing, but he hadn't given up Peter, and consequently he was constantly getting entangled in his unsurrendered self.

We must be careful to understand that self-surrender does not mean self-extinction. You can never get rid of the self. If you put it out through the door, it will come back through the window. The self is the eternal part of human personality. It is that which makes you a person, which gives you individuality. A selfless person would be a contradiction in terms. You can be unselfish, yes, but never selfless.

Self-surrender is a radical shift from self-centeredness to Christ-centeredness, so that life is no longer revolving around oneself, but around Christ. We must take that letter *I* and bend it around until it becomes a zero or an *O*. Then the word SIN will be changed to SON. When the unsurrendered I or ego bends itself to the Master's will, this leads to true sonship in Christ.

We pointed out previously that when the prodigal son left home the words on his lips were: "Give me—give me." We now observe that when he returned home, the words on his lips were these: "Make me—make me." The center had shifted from himself to his father.

When we study English grammar, we learn how to conjugate a verb thus: First person, *I;* second person, *you;* third person, *he.* I make; you make; he makes. But in self-surrender our spiritual grammar must be reversed. First person, *He;* second person, *you;* third person, *I.* God must be first in my life; He must have the preeminence. You, my neighbor, must be next.

There are basically two patterns of life: one revolving around self as the center, and the other revolving around God as the center. The New Testament symbolically speaks of these patterns as "the old man" and "the new man." All of the events and stuff of which life is made fall into one or the other of these two patterns. Indeed, to some extent in unsurrendered hearts these patterns exist simultaneously, overlapping, so that when pictured geometrically there is an elipse where a circle ought to be.

In his book entitled *The Spirit of Holiness,* Dr. Everett Cattell illustrates this common spiritual condition by passing a horseshoe magnet under a sheet of paper on which have been sprinkled iron filings. Looking from above one cannot see the magnet, but one can tell the location of its poles by the behavior of the filings, which instantly arrange themselves around the poles and form two overlapping patterns. "In the lives of converted men," suggests Dr. Cattell, "there are still two great poles—self and God. All of the particles that go to make up life group themselves around these two poles in patterns of life which are partially self-centered and partially God-centered. It is conceivable that the particles where the patterns overlap have a hard time making up their minds as to which pole to obey."

We must be cleansed of self-centeredness. This duality of pattern must go out of existence. The self as a pole apart from God must yield up its aloofness, its separateness, its enmity against God, its independent sovereignty, by an act of utter surrender. It must move over and become hid with Christ in God. The self then continues to live, but it lives in God. The poles are now—so to speak—identical, and the pattern of life is one—integrated.

This spiritual paradox is most concisely and intriguingly expressed by Paul in his oft quoted words, "I have been crucified with Christ; [nevertheless I live;] it is no longer I who live, but Christ who lives in me; and the life I now live in the flesh I live by faith in the Son of God, who loved me and gave himself for me" (Gal. 2:20). This is an amazing verse. It emphasizes self-surrender, or self-crucifixion, and yet at the same time it speaks so much of the self. The personal pronouns are prominent. But we must follow Paul carefully in his line of reasoning.

It is evident he is speaking about three different egos, or more correctly, three facets of the one ego. "I have been crucified with Christ," he begins. This is the part of the ego that needs crucifixion. It is that proud, perverse, self-centered ego which always seeks to glorify itself. The only cure for this is crucifixion, a "death to self." Then Paul goes on, "Nevertheless I live" (a phrase occurring in the King James version). This is the part of the self which lives on after the crucifixion. It is our essential selfhood, the real self, imperishable, eternal. God himself has created it and He will not destroy it. It will live on forever. "It is no longer I who live, but Christ who lives in me," Paul concludes. Herein lies the secret. When the carnal, self-centered ego is crucified, then there can be a true self filled and possessed by Christ. It becomes a Christ-centered ego. Thus Paul in one breath said, "I am dead," and in the next breath says, "I am alive." Then he qualifies that by saying, "It is really Christ who is living in me." It's a death that leads to life.

There is the story of a man who was glancing over the obituary section of the morning newspaper when, to his surprise, he found his own name in the list. He looked again. Sure enough, the initials, name, and address were all correct. He was reported as dead. At first he laughed over the matter, but soon the telephone began ringing, as many of his stunned friends sought to inquire about his sudden death. Finally, he became irritated and called up the newspaper editor. "Sir," he said, "you have reported my death in the morning paper, but I'm very much alive. It's causing a lot of confusion among my friends. I demand you set this right!"

The editor was at first nonplussed and apologetic, but then in a flash of inspiration he said, "Don't worry, Sir. I'll make things right. Tomorrow I'll put your name in the birth column!"

This is a spiritual parable. If we die out to the old carnal self, then suddenly we will find ourselves alive in Christ—alive as never before. For after the crucifixion comes the resurrection. The old self dies and a new self arises. We put our names in the death column and immediately we find them placed in the birth column.

A note of warning needs to be sounded at this point. The crucifixion of the old self that we have been emphasizing cannot be brought about the individual himself. That is, self cannot crucify itself. It is irrevocably opposed to its own crucifixion. The only thing the individual can do is to *become willing* for the self to be crucified by the Holy Spirit, who alone is the Executioner. As Paul clearly states, "No man can say 'Jesus is Lord' except by the Holy Spirit" (I Cor. 12:3). But when we are willing, then we find He is able.

Receive the Fullness of the Spirit

The full surrender of the self is not an end in itself. It is merely clearing the channel so that the Spirit may give himself in His fullness. This must not, however, be interpreted as a form of celestial bargaining, whereby we give our all and in exchange He gives His all. By a full surrender we are not in any sense making ourselves worthy to receive the fullness of the Spirit. No one is worthy, but all Christians are eligible. This is God's gift, and it is for the asking. Jesus said, "If you then, who are evil, know how to give good gifts to your children, how much more will the heavenly Father give the Holy Spirit to those who ask him!" (Luke 11:13) All we need to do is to ask the Holy Spirit who lives in us to take full control and sanctify and fill.

In seeking the fullness of the Holy Spirit, our eyes must be upon the Giver himself, and not upon one of the gifts. Paul makes it clear that the Holy Spirit distributes His gifts "to each one individually as he wills" (I Cor. 12:11). All do not receive the same gift; neither does any person possess all of the gifts. We cannot dictate to the Holy Spirit what gift He shall give us. This is His prerogative. We can, however, all receive the gift of the fullness of the Holy Spirit himself. The promise is unto all!

It was shortly after my wife and I arrived in India to begin our missionary career that the Japanese attacked Pearl

Harbor and drew the United States into World War II. Within a few months, Japanese forces had advanced to the borders of India, and the U.S. ambassador was urging all American citizens to evacuate. My wife and six-month-old daughter returned by troop transport to the United States, but I remained behind on the field. It was two years and seven months before we were reunited.

During the long period of separation my wife and I suffered many hours of loneliness. My wife wrote to me regularly, but in those war years mail was slow and the censorship was strict. Often whole sections of a letter were cut out. At times she mailed me a parcel with some special gift as a token of her love. On one occasion while I was holding special revival meetings in Calcutta, a thief broke into the parsonage and, among other household articles, stole my best suit and fountain pen. When my wife heard of the loss, with her meager savings she bought me a new suit and fountain pen, and mailed them out to me in India. I was, of course, delighted to receive the gift. But I wrote to her and said, "Dearest, I thank you for all your letters which assure me of your love and prayers. I thank you for all the parcels, and especially for this most recent one. But, Darling, I am getting to the place where I am not satisfied with just letters and parcels. I long for you and you alone. If I could just look into your face and hold you in my arms, that would be worth more than thousands of letters and parcels. The next time you send me a parcel, just wrap yourself up and come out!"

There came a time in my spiritual life when I had to say much the same thing to the Holy Spirit. I said in my heart, "Lord, I thank You for all your gifts—for forgiveness, for peace, for comfort and strength. But, Lord, I want more than just gifts. I want only You. I want You to permeate and fill every part of my being."

We must desire the Lord more than anything else in the whole world. We must want Him and Him alone.

Finally we must receive the Holy Spirit in His fullness *by faith*. Peter said before the council in Jerusalem, "And God who knows the heart bore witness to them, giving them the Holy Spirit just as he did to us; and he made no distinction between us and them, but cleansed their hearts *by faith*" (Acts 15:8-9, italics mine). All the gifts of God are received by faith.

Many Christians seem to surrender themselves, to die out to self, but it's all so morbid, so depressing. They're surrendered, but empty. They need to take the positive step of faith. Surrender says, "I am crucified with Christ." Faith says, "Christ lives in me." Surrender says, "Empty and cleansed." Faith says, "Filled and fitted for the Master's use." Surrender says, "I give my all." Faith says, "I receive Your all."

Faith is merely taking God at His word, letting my whole weight down on His promises. He assures us that the Gift of the Holy Spirit is for all; that He gives the Holy Spirit to those who ask Him; that if we shall ask anything in His name, He will grant it. So I say in my heart, "Lord, I know what You say is true. I now ask to be filled with the Spirit, and I believe that You fill me at this moment. Thank You, Lord."

Since this experience is entered into by faith, it can happen in our lives anytime, anywhere, when we ask and believe.

In a certain church I was giving a series of messages on the subject of the Holy Spirit. A young housewife, a sincere child of God, became hungry for the fullness of the Spirit. One morning, all alone in the house, she was working in the kitchen. In her mind, however, she was meditating and praying. Suddenly she lifted her eyes and said aloud, "Lord, the preacher said we can receive the baptism with the Holy Spirit by faith. This, I see, is in accordance with Your Word. So, Lord, right here and now I ask You to fill me with the

Holy Spirit, and I believe You do." In the evening service she stood and testified that she had the inner assurance that the Holy Spirit had filled her. It happened while she was in the kitchen, washing the breakfast dishes!

A few years ago, at a quiet retreat for preachers and laymen in New York state, I delivered the same series of messages on the Holy Spirit. At the end of the first session, time was given for questions and discussion. The ministers became involved in the theological pros and cons of the subject. Suddenly a layman, whose first name was Sam, interrupted the discussion and called out. "I don't follow all this theological jargon. All I know is that I need the fullness of the Holy Spirit. Tell me how I can find it." So I briefly outlined the steps of self-surrender and faith.

When the evening session was over, the leader of the retreat explained that we would now begin a period of silence until the morning devotional period. He also informed us that on our way out we should pick up a card containing the name of one of the persons present at the retreat. We were to pray for that person in particular before retiring for the night. Immediately I said in my heart, "Lord, give me Sam as my prayer partner." When I picked up my card and looked at the name, it read "Sam ———." Coincidence, you say. But that would be difficult in a stack of approximately 100 cards. I felt it was providence. I went to my room and prayed earnestly for Sam, that he might be filled with the Spirit.

In the morning we all gathered for corporate, silent devotions. At the end of the period, Sam jumped to his feet and said excitedly, "I could hardly wait for the silence to be broken. I am bursting to share the good news with you. Last night the Lord filled me with the Holy Spirit. I asked and believed, and the Lord answered my prayer." It happened while he was taking a shower!

Many years have passed since a tall, lanky, redheaded

Kentuckian, a civil engineer student in the University of Cincinnati, was walking down the sidewalk on Clifton Avenue near the university campus. It was a cold, dreary evening in January. The previous summer at Sychar Camp Meeting in Mount Vernon, Ohio, this young man had been converted and called to go to India as a missionary. Recently he had received instruction concerning the baptism with the Holy Spirit and was earnestly seeking the experience. Walking along the sidewalk, deep in thought, he said audibly, "Lord, I have placed my ambitions, my career, my marriage, my all on the altar. What more should I do to receive the Holy Spirit in His fullness? This is what I need and desire more than anything else." An inner voice said quietly, "Just ask and believe." So the young man—my father—lifted his eyes heavenward and said from the depths of his heart, "Lord, I do believe. Fill me now!"

Not long ago my father took me to Cincinnati and pointed out the spot where it happened. We stood there and shared in a time of thanksgiving and prayer.

I remember in my own life, when I was a student at Asbury College in Wilmore, Ky., how I first received the fullness of the Spirit. I had been a Christian for about two years and had started out very zealously in my Christian life. But then I seemed to hit a plateau. I was making little progress spiritually. I was deeply distressed at the discovery of certain attitudes and desires in my heart that were clearly contrary to the spirit of Christ. I was a divided person; there was civil war within. The doctrine of the Holy Spirit and sanctification was not new to me. I had been reared in the Wesleyan tradition. All I needed was to appropriate the truth personally and turn doctrine into experience. Then one morning, sitting alone at the desk in my private devotions, I prayed silently within myself, "Lord, You said, 'Blessed are those who hunger and thirst for righteousness, for they shall be satisfied.' Well, I'm hungry now. I'm thirsty. I want to be cleansed and filled with the Spirit more than anything else. Lord, fulfil Your promise now. I believe." At that moment I felt as if I had had a good bath. I felt clean all over. And there was the assurance that the Holy Spirit had taken possession of my being. Sad to say, I haven't always been faithful to the Master. There was a time when I miserably failed my Lord and lost the assurance of His fullness. But the Spirit was faithful in His ministry of conviction and discipline and brought me back to the place of full surrender and faith. The assurance of His fullness is real today.

These then are the steps to the Spirit-filled life. Surrender yourself completely to His will and die to the old self. Receive Him in His fullness by faith. Realize that it is God's intention to fill you with His Spirit. Make it your intention to be filled. Then the promise will pass into fulfillment in your life, and Pentecost will be as real to you as it was to the disciples in the Upper Room at Jerusalem.

7

Love Is the Sign

The greatest statement in all human language is, "God is love." Not just, "God loves," but, "God *is* love." He is the personification of love. Love is the very fiber of His being.

All the acts of God spring from this basic fact. For example, love is the basis of His creative action. Why did God create? Because love involves relationship. It requires objects upon which it can lavish its affection. And so God created man in order that He might enter into loving relationship with him, and that He might pour out His love upon him. Parents create for the same reason. They desire children whom they can call their very own, upon whom they can shower their love, and who in turn will respond in love.

Love is the basis of God's redemptive action. "For God so loved the world that he gave his only Son, that whoever believes in him should not perish but have eternal life" (John 3:16). "In this the love of God was made manifest among us, that God sent his only Son into the world, so that we might live through him" (I John 4:9). "By this we know love, that he laid down his life for us" (I John 3:16). It was a dangerous thing for God to create. His creatures might go wrong and break His heart. But God took this chance. He knew He would have to lay His love alongside the sin of man. The Cross was, therefore, inherent in creation. Jesus was called the Lamb slain from the foundation of the world (Rev. 13:8). Not just 2,000 years ago. The moment man disobeyed and became a sinner, a cross was formed in God's heart. This was inevitable. But how could we know that God cared, that He suffered on account of our sin? The only way was for Him to lift up a cross at some point in history for all men to see. Through the outer, wooden cross on Calvary, we see the inner, invisible cross in the heart of God. And so because God is love, He loved the world and gave His Son, and the Son gave His life.

Love is also the basis of our approach to God. Suppose I were a sinner in need of help and guidance, and came to you for advice. You might say to me, "God is *omnipotent.* Go to Him, and He will help you." But I dare not go to God on the basis of His omnipotence. I am frail and finite. He may crush me in His mighty hand. Again, you might say, "God is *omniscient.* Go to Him and He will help you." I dare not approach God on the basis of His omniscience, for He knows all about me—every act I have committed, every word I have spoken, even my innermost thoughts and desires.

Then suppose you say, "God is *holy.* Go to Him for help." But I dare not approach Him on the basis of His holiness. He is Absolute Perfection, while I am a miserable sinner. The closer I get to Him, the greater is my embarrassment. Again you say, "God is *just.* Go to Him for help." But I dare not approach Him on the basis of His justice. I have sinned against Him, and stand guilty in His presence. Justice demands that I be condemned for my sin.

Finally, you say to me, "'God is *love';* go to Him and He will have compassion on you." Then I forget my embarrassment, my unworthiness, and I rush into His outstretched arms, pleading His mercy. And because He loves me, He will welcome, pardon, cleanse, and receive me. Love is the only basis upon which I can approach Him.

Since love is one of the basic characteristics of God, it is, therefore, one of the basic characteristics of the Spirit-filled life. This is the truth that Paul emphasizes in his First Epistle to the Corinthian church. Having discussed the various gifts of the Spirit in chapter 12, he concludes by saying, "I will show you a still more excellent way." Then in chapter 13 he gives us his great tribute to love, some of the most magnificent words in Scripture and in all literature.

If I speak in the tongues of men and of angels, but have not love, I am a noisy gong or a clanging cymbal. And if I have prophetic powers, and understand all mysteries and all knowledge, and if I have all faith so as to remove mountains, but have not love, I am nothing. If I give away all I have, and if I deliver my body to be burned, but have not love, I gain nothing (I Cor. 13:1-3).

In essence Paul is saying: We may proclaim the most wonderful words; we may possess the most marvelous gifts; we may perform the most noble deeds. But if we do not possess and practice love, we are nothing. All is in vain.

This is the reason why Jesus, when questioned, declared that the greatest commandment of all is to love—to love God supremely and to love our neighbors sincerely.

"The first [commandment] is, 'Hear, O Israel: The Lord our God, the Lord is one; and you shall love the Lord your God with all your heart, and with all your soul, and with all your mind, and with all your strength.' The second is this, 'You shall love your neighbor as yourself.' There is no other commandment greater than these" (Mark 12:29-31).

Since God is love and man is made in the image of God, it follows that man is created with the capacity to love. Previously psychologists used to say that there were three basic urges in man—self, sex, and the herd: the desire for self-preservation, the desire for self-propagation, and the desire to be in the company of others. But in recent years psychologists have been insisting that there is really only one basic human urge, and that is the desire to love and to be loved. Man must love something. If he doesn't love God and his neighbor, he will at least love art, music, literature, sports, his country, or a good cause. This is why we commonly remark, "Love makes the world go round."

The opposite of that adage is also true: "The lack of love makes the world go wrong." The basic cause for many broken homes and for much of our juvenile delinquency today is right at this point. Many husbands and wives have lost their first love. Many sons and daughters have not experienced true love (which includes discipline) in the home. Many young people who run off and get married at an early age are really seeking for love which they did not receive from their parents.

I remember reading in an Illinois newspaper a few years ago about the abduction of a three-week-old baby in Metropolis, in the southern part of the state. A woman in her late thirties called on the parents of the child and identified herself as the representative of the Massac Memorial Hospital. She claimed the baby had been selected as "baby of the month," and said she wanted to take it to the hospital for a photograph. When she hadn't returned after several hours, the frantic mother phoned the hospital, then the police. The abductor was discovered with the baby in Chicago a few days later. When the authorities asked her why she stole the baby, she replied tearfully, "I just wanted something to love." Then it was discovered that within the past month both her husband and father had died, and she herself had suffered a miscarriage, and now she was left with no children of her own. So in desperation she stole the baby in order to have "something to love."

So religion and psychology both say, "You shall love." This is basic in the Christian life. But someone asks, How can you command love? Love is not really genuine unless it is spontaneous—from the heart. The answer is, when God *commands* love, human nature *commends* it. If we violate the law of love, we violate the law of our being. If we don't love God and our neighbor, we can't really love ourselves. Suppose I am addressing a group of people, and at noon I say to them, "Go to lunch now." That would be in the nature of a command, but there would be something within each person that would respond to the order. In like manner, when Christ requires us to love, our inner nature responds to the demand, for we were endowed with the capacity to love.

Then Jesus goes on to say, "You shall love the Lord your God." God is to be the Object of our love—a Person, not merely a doctrine, or an idea, or just a cause. This is to be a personal relationship.

God is the *perfect Object* of our love. He is absolutely good and holy, with no faults or defects. He is completely dependable and will never let us down. Sometimes my wife says to me, "Honey, I love you in spite of all your faults." And I can say the same to her. As human beings we all have our faults. We have to love one another in spite of our weaknesses and shortcomings. But we can't look into the face of God and say, "Lord, I love You in spite of Your faults." He has none. He is the one Person in all the universe who is absolutely perfect and dependable.

God is also the *eternal Object* of our love. This is a loving relationship that has no end. In the world of human relationships, there comes a time when we lay husband, wife, child, or friend in the grave, and the former intimate relationship of love is broken. But when we fall in love with Christ, this is the beginning of an eternal romance. For neither height nor depth, principalities nor powers, not even death itself can separate us from the love of Christ (Rom. 8:38-39).

A small boy had a pet rabbit which his father gave him for a birthday gift. He dearly loved the rabbit and carried it around with him wherever he went. But one day a couple of stray dogs pounced on the pet and tore it into shreds. The boy's heart was broken and he wept for days. Then his father presented him with a beautiful puppy, and soon the lad forgot all about the rabbit. He cuddled his dog and played with it for hours at a time. It followed at his heels wherever he went. But one day while playing, the puppy ran across the street after a ball, and was killed instantly by a swiftly passing car. Again the boy's heart was broken and he wept profusely over the loss of his second pet. He climbed up on his father's lap and through his tears cried out, "Daddy, my rabbit is gone and my puppy is gone. Can't you get me something to love which won't ever die?"

There is something in the heart of man that cries out in similar vein: Isn't there something or someone in the universe that I can love, who will never die? Yes, there is Someone. The Lord Jesus Christ. When we fall in love with Him, we fall in love forever. This is an eternal romance.

Then Jesus goes on to say, "You shall love the Lord your God with all your heart, and with all your soul, and with all your mind, and with all your strength." He emphasizes the word "all." Our love for God is to be *complete*. He desires *all* our devotion. Isn't this true of us also? The wife wants all of her husband's love; the husband wants all of his wife's love. We are not satisfied until we have all. Can God be satisfied with anything less?

Our love for God is to be a *well-balanced love*, expressing every aspect of our personality. We are to love Him with all our *heart*, with all *the sincerity of our emotional nature*. We are to love Him with all our *mind*, with all *the sanity of our intellectual nature*. We are to love Him with all our *soul*, with all *the intensity of our volitional nature*. We are to love Him with all our *strength*, with all *the vitality of our physical nature*. The whole of man is to be brought under the sway of God. This makes for unified personality, for fixation of purpose.

Many are loving God in an unbalanced and, therefore, weak way. There are those who love Him with the strength of the feelings and weakness of the mind. This makes the *emotionalist* in religion. Some love with the strength of the emotions and weakness of the will. This makes the *sentimentalist* in religion. Others love Him with the strength of the mind and weakness of the emotions. This makes the *intellectualist* in religion. Still others love Him with the strength of the will and weakness of the emotions. This produces the *legalist* in religion, the man of iron—very moral, but unloving and unlovable. The really strong Christian is the one who loves with the strength of the mind, the strength of the emotions, the strength of the will, and the strength of the whole personality. The entire being is caught up in a passion of love and self-surrender to Christ.

Jesus follows the first great commandment—love God with your whole being—with a second commandment: "Love your neighbor as yourself." The two cannot be separated. They are like the two rails of the railroad track or like the two wings of a bird. To talk of loving God without loving our fellowman is a farce. It would be comparable to putting our arms around a person and then kicking him in the shins. Spell Christian love with a capital *L*. The vertical stroke, representing our relationship to God, is immediately followed by a horizontal stroke, which represents our relationship to our fellowmen. If we love God, we will love people.

My father spent his adolescent years in Tucson, Ariz. While he was a student in high school, one summer vacation he worked on the levee near the Mexican border. It was there that for the first time he saw Indians from southern Asia. Several men had come over to Mexico at the invitation of the government to work as day laborers on certain public projects. When my father saw these Hindu "coolies" with their caste-marks and strange customs, and heard their weird music around the campfire at night, he said to himself, These people are the offscouring of the earth. They are the most loathsome people I have ever seen. Little did he realize that within a few years he would receive a call from God to serve as a missionary in India! But before this latter event he was converted at Camp Sychar in Ohio and then later filled with the Holy Spirit. He received such a baptism of love in his heart that his attitude toward the Indians was completely transformed. India became his beloved country; the people of India became his own. It can truthfully be said that no one loved India, nor was anyone loved by the Indians, more than my father.

A few years ago I was conducting a one-day ashram in an Episcopalian church in Baltimore, Md. An attractive university coed came to the retreat, but when she saw a good number of Negroes present, she became resentful and almost decided to go back home. However, she exercised self-restraint and remained. She listened attentively to the messages on the Holy Spirit, and when the invitation was given to come forward and pray at the altar, she readily responded to the call. In the closing session she stood before the group, confessed her resentment, and asked the Negroes present to forgive her. Then with a note of excitement in her voice, she said, "You know, I asked God to fill me with the Holy Spirit, and He answered my prayer. Now I suddenly find that my attitude of race prejudice is gone, and for the first time I am able to love everybody, even my black brothers and sisters." From rejection to acceptance within the period of six hours! It was truly a miracle of God's grace.

I am writing this chapter in the heart of the Congo in Africa, where I am attending the annual conference of the Methodist church. There is a young missionary here, Paul Law, and his lovely wife, who recently graduated from Asbury College. They have come to minister to the Congolese people. Six years ago Paul's father, Burleigh Law, missionary-pilot of the Methodist church, was shot and killed by rebels during the civil war that took place. He is buried on the mission station at Wembo Nyama. Today his son, Paul, is back at the same station, preaching Christ to the people of the area. Humanly speaking, one would expect Paul Law to feel ill will toward the people of Congo for murdering his father. One would think that he would never want to see Congo again. But here he is, back at the scene of his father's martydom, loving and serving in the name of Christ. Nothing but the love of Christ could help a man to do that.

In his letter to the church at Rome, Paul states that "God's love has been poured into our hearts through the Holy Spirit which has been given to us" (Rom. 5:5). Then in the Galatian Epistle he writes that "the fruit of the Spirit is love, joy, peace, patience, kindness, goodness, faithfulness, gentleness, self-control" (Gal. 5:22-23). Thus love with all its various manifestations is the supreme evidence of the indwelling presence of the Holy Spirit. And when we are completely yielded to Christ and filled with the Spirit, His love is evident in our lives in even greater measure.

The gifts of the Spirit are important and should be used for the edification of the Church and for the glory of God. But the Holy Spirit distributes the various gifts according to His own will. To one He gives the gift of prophecy (or proclamation), to another the gift of healing, to another the gift of discernment, to another the gift of tongues, and so on (see I Cor. 12:4-11, 27-31). No one person possesses all nine gifts; neither do we all have identically the same gift. Therefore we cannot claim that any one particular gift is the evidence of the baptism with the Spirit. However, every Spirit-filled person possesses *all* the *fruits* of the Spirit. The Holy Spirit doesn't give one person love, another person patience, another person peace, and so on. Each one of us needs all these Christian graces. We all need "love, joy, peace, patience, kindness, goodness, faithfulness, gentleness, self-control."

The fruit of the Spirit is the supreme evidence of the Spirit's indwelling presence. It is significant that the fullness of the Spirit was first granted on the Day of Pentecost, which was a Jewish agricultural festival commemorating the first-fruits of the harvest. The baptism with the Holy Spirit is a spiritual festival, producing the fruit of the Spirit in our lives. And love is the chief characteristic of the fruit, for all other graces are merely manifestations of love. Joy is the emotional expression of love. Peace is love in repose. Patience and gentleness are love in behavior. Goodness and meekness are the disposition of love. Faith is the quiet confidence of love. Temperance is love in control.

One of the greatest needs of the Church today is a new baptism of love. It is only when God's divine love is "poured into our hearts" (Rom. 5:5) that we will be able to see every man as a person for whom Christ died and as a potential child of God. Then only will we be able to "love one another earnestly from the heart" (I Pet. 1:22), and will men know that we are truly Christ's disciples.

When Jesus appeared before His disciples for the third time after the Resurrection, He prepared a fire on the shore of the Tiberias Sea and served them bread and fish for supper. After the meal He spoke personally to Peter. This was the Master's final examination of this rugged fisherman, who had been a student in His walking seminary for the previous three years. There were three questions on the exam and all three were essentially the same. "Simon, son of John, do you love me?" And the record tells us that Peter was grieved when the Lord repeated the question for the third time. For he suddenly remembered a similar scene just a few weeks previously when, warming himself at a fire, he had denied his Lord three times. He had miserably failed to take his stand for Christ, for his love was vacillating and weakened by fear of men. Now his Lord was demanding a love that was constant and complete. But there came a time in Peter's life, on the Day of Pentecost, when his love for Christ was strengthened with a moral fiber that sent him out ready to face a hostile world and willing to lay down his life in the Master's service.

Notice that every time Peter answered the Lord's question, the Lord immediately told him to take care of His lambs and sheep. In other words, our love for Christ must be expressed in service to our fellowman. Love is not a passive emotion that folds its hands and sits in quiet contemplation. Love is aggressive action, ready to roll up its sleeves and dirty its hands in ministering to needy people.

In elaborating upon His command to love our "neighbors," Jesus gave the story of the Good Samaritan. He emphasized that love does not sit on the sidelines as a spectator, wagging its head in a mild form of pity. Love is willing to get down off its position of comfort and privilege and become involved in the sufferings and struggles of needy people. The Samaritan traveler not only had compassion on the man lying in the ditch, but he got off his horse, went to the man, bound up his wounds, took him to the nearest inn, and even paid the bill! Love always expresses itself in action and in self-giving.

The Master today is giving each of us the same examination and exhortation: "Do you love me more than these? . . . [Then] Feed my sheep." He is commanding each one of us: Love God supremely and love your neighbor sincerely. But this is possible only when we have experienced a personal Pentecost in our lives and the marvelous love of God is poured into our hearts by the Holy Spirit.

We need to pray in the words of the hymnwriter:

> *Teach me to love Thee as Thine angels love,*
> *One holy passion filling all my frame;*
> *The kindling of the heaven-descended Dove,*
> *My heart an altar, and Thy love the flame.*

8

Keep Walking

There are two major fallacies concerning sanctification or the Spirit-filled life. One is the idea that the fullness of the Spirit is the result of spiritual growth and, therefore, a gradual process. We have already pointed out that, though there may be certain steps preparing us for the baptism with the Holy Spirit, we can never really grow or slide into the experience. There comes a time in our Christian lives when we realize our inner need for a deeper work of the Spirit, we make a full surrender of ourselves, and trust God to fill us with the Holy Spirit. This is as definite a crisis as conversion or the new birth.

However, it is just as fallacious to look upon the fullness of the Spirit as *only* a crisis, resulting in a fixed or final condition of existence, beyond which there is no room for growth. The Spirit-filled life is both a crisis and a process. After we have been sanctified by the Spirit, we still must grow in grace until we reach spiritual maturity and the full stature of Christ. Like Paul, we must constantly press on to perfection (Phil. 3:12).

The Christian life is not fixed or static. It is dynamic and progressive. What the Holy Spirit fills, He expands. He is the divine "wind," the "breath of God," filling us, and thus expanding us. We maintain the fullness by never settling down in a static level of holiness, but by continuously receiving His infilling. In the nineteenth chapter of Acts we read how Paul challenged the Ephesian disciples to receive the baptism with the Holy Spirit and how they entered into a great crisis experience (Acts 19:1-7). But later, in his Epistle to the Ephesians, he exhorts them to be continuously filled with the Spirit (Eph. 5:18). This is the force of the Greek tense he uses—the present imperative—which literally may be translated, *"Be being filled* with the Spirit." The Spirit-filled life is not like a vessel filled to the brim with water and left standing somewhere. We are to be channels of spiritual blessing to a needy world. We are as a vessel placed under a running faucet, so that the water is constantly flowing in and flowing out, while the vessel remains full at all times.

The Spirit-filled life is primarily a relationship to the Holy Spirit. As long as we maintain this intimate relationship, He will keep on cleansing and empowering us from day to day, and the fruit of the Spirit will be evident in our lives. The moment we mar this relationship, the Spirit is hindered from perfecting His work in us, and we are in spiritual danger.

How is the Spirit-filled life to be maintained? In exactly the same way that the fullness of the Spirit is received for the first time—by self-surrender and faith. The initial act must now become a perennial attitude. The crisis must become a daily walk.

ATTITUDE OF SURRENDER

Like sanctification, self-surrender is both a crisis and a process. There comes a moment when we surrender completely for the first time in our lives, but then that act of surrender must be followed by a day-by-day attitude of surrender and obedience. It's like the marriage relationship. At the altar we say one big "Yes" which determines the direction of our whole lives. "Forsaking all others, I take this woman [this man] as my wedded wife [husband], in sickness or in health, for better or for worse, till death do us part." But then, those of us who are married know that there are a lot of little yeses to say down through the years, as husband and wife relate to one another in all types of situations and trials.

There is a sense in which we have to make a new surrender from time to time. Just because we are fully surrendered to God at this moment does not mean that we will never discover new areas for surrender down the line. The light which the Holy Spirit shines into our hearts is not so much like a searchlight, suddenly turned on full power, revealing every single item in our lives that is contrary to His will. That would probably overpower and frighten us to death. The Spirit works more like a rheostat, turning up the light gradually. As it becomes brighter and brighter it exposes new areas that need to be adjusted to His will. Since we have already said the big "Yes" at the altar of surrender, we now immediately and willingly follow with another "Yes, Lord, I surrender this too." In gratitude we say, "Lord, I didn't realize this defect in my life. Thank You for showing it to me. I am ready to obey."

In India there was a village Christian who was respected for his piety and exemplary life. He was poor and illiterate, and wore only a *dhoti* (cotton wrap-around), and a blanket thrown over his shoulder. But he was truly a converted man and filled with the Spirit. One year at the annual camp meeting he gave his testimony. He told how just recently he had been resting in the shade of a mango tree, meditating and praying, when an inner voice said to him, "Jettiyappa, I have something against you."

"What is it, Lord?" he asked.

"Jettiyappa, you smoke," the inner voice continued. "I could use you more effectively if you would be willing to give up this habit."

Immediately Jettiyappa responded, "Lord, I didn't

realize I was displeasing You by this habit. Thank You for revealing this to me." And so saying, he threw away his bundle of country-made cigarettes and never smoked again.

In like manner, from time to time the Holy Spirit will speak to us and lead us on to new depths of surrender. If we are sincerely walking in the light, we will be sensitive to His promptings and respond quickly in obedience.

Dr. H. C. Morrison, for many years president of Asbury College, used to say that consecration is always in two bundles—the bundle of the *known* and the bundle of the *unknown*. We have to place both bundles on the altar. We surrender all that we are aware of at the present and all that is to come in the future. Thus, consecration is not like writing on a sheet of paper a list of all the things that we are turning over to God and then signing our names at the bottom. It is like signing our names at the bottom of a blank sheet, handing it over to the Lord, and saying, "Here, Lord, You fill it in. It may take You five years or 50 years, but I am ready to accept Your will at all times."

When we talk about self-surrender, we really mean a commitment of our wills to Jesus Christ. We put our willingness into His hands. But we are not actually surrendering anything concrete until we face the particular issue at hand. Psychologically speaking, it is impossible to surrender anything of which we are not aware. At the moment we can only affirm our willingness to decide in God's favor whenever we become aware of some specific issues before us. We say to God, "Lord, I renounce the right to make my choices on the basis of my own plans and desires. In every event I will always seek to know and to do Your will." But the content of that will and the practical outworking of that willingness in the daily arena of life are things we will be dealing with the rest of our lives. As each new crisis arises we will have to reaffirm our initial surrender by saying, "Lord, I choose Your will now in this particular situation."

It is right at this point that we sometimes have problems, however. As we face each specific situation, there can still be a struggle between our emotions and our wills. Feelings and desires can give us a rough time. Sometimes the battle may be severe. We may be tempted to feel that we never really made a full surrender in the first place. But the best thing to do in such circumstances is to face our feelings with complete honesty and tell God what these feelings are. Then by the help of the Holy Spirit we surrender to His will in the particular situation. We ratify, as it were, our original treaty with Him. Victory continues to be ours.

Perhaps the finest biblical illustration of this truth is found in the life of Jesus himself. Few, if any, of us could ever fully grasp the tremendous struggle that took place in His heart and mind as He prayed in the Garden of Gethsemane on the night of His arrest. Three times Jesus threw himself on the ground, we are told, and prayed in desperate agony. "His sweat became like great drops of blood falling down upon the ground" (Luke 22:44). Remember that just a short while before He had said to His disciples, "Let not your hearts be troubled." And now the Gospel writer tells us that he "began to be greatly distressed and troubled" (Mark 14:33). Jesus himself said to His disciples, "My soul is very sorrowful, even to death" (v. 34).

Why all the struggle? Hadn't Jesus from the very beginning of His life and ministry made a total surrender of himself into the hands of the Father? Didn't He affirm over and over again, "My will is to do the will of My Father"? Is there any question about the reality and depth of His surrender? Absolutely not. But there was a terrific struggle between the emotions of the moment and His will. There was the natural human aversion to death. There was the natural shrinking from the excruciating pain and shame of the Cross. There was the horrifying realization that He was about to bear the sin of the world.

It is interesting to note that Jesus accepted His own emotions and struggles without any embarrassment. Even the Gospel writers made no attempt to hide them. But Jesus won the victory when He finally prayed, "Not my will, but thine, be done." At that moment He reconfirmed the attitude of obedience and surrender that He had maintained from the very beginning. So He "in every respect has been tempted as we are, yet without sinning" (Heb. 4:15).

Who is there among us, even the most mature child of God, that has not gone through a similar experience? We all need to be as honest about our own inner struggles as the New Testament is concerning the struggles of Jesus. Young Christians must not get the false impression that surrender is something that we do once and for all and that's the end of the matter. We can make a lifelong commitment. We can say, "I surrender all," and mean every word of it. But to put this commitment into practice, to actualize it, to make it real in concrete situations is a continuous, lifetime affair. Again and again, in each new crisis, we have to say, "Not my will, but thine, be done." But this is where the growing process takes place. We become stronger in our commitment, we become more sensitive to His leadings, as we become more mature in our spiritual lives.

In Arabia, certain horses are trained especially for the service of the king. The primary lesson is that of obedience. For example, whenever the trainer blows his whistle a certain way, the horses must learn to run toward him. The training goes on for months, and then a very interesting test is given. For several days the horses are deprived of water, until they become frantic with thirst and pace excitedly around the fenced-in area. Then suddenly the gate leading to the pond is opened, and the horses rush toward the water to quench their thirst. But just as they are about to drink, the trainer blows his whistle. The horses instinctively stop where they are. A tremendous struggle goes on within them. There is the maddening desire to stoop and drink, but their wills have been trained to obey the sound of the whistle. Those horses which turn away from the water at this critical moment and run back to the trainer are the only ones considered fit for the service of the king. In like manner, those children of God who have learned to be sensitive to the leadings of the Spirit and to obey the will of the Father at all times are the only ones fit for the service of the King of Kings.

Attitude of Faith

We receive the fullness of the Holy Spirit by faith. We realize it is God's desire to fill us with the Spirit, so we take Him at His word and let our whole weight down upon His promises. We reach out the hand of faith and accept the gift. This is a definite act of the will, resulting in a crisis experience. But from then on we must maintain this attitude of faith from day to day. So faith, like surrender, is a process as well as a crisis. It is a constant attitude as well as a definite act. It is a disposition of the mind as well as a decision of the will.

The temptation will arise to doubt the validity of our experience. This is especially true if we permit our faith to be influenced by our emotions. Our feelings often fluctuate. They vary according to daily circumstances, our temperaments and moods, and even the weather. They are, consequently, a very shaky foundation for our faith.

Suppose one day the weather is bad, everything seems to go wrong, and, on top of it all, I am afflicted with a severe migraine headache. I say to myself, I don't feel very good today. I don't think I'm married anymore. Ridiculous, you say. You're right. What has the fact of my married status to do with the way I feel at any given moment? But is this any more foolish than saying to myself on a cold, rainy day, when everything seems to be adverse, "I don't think I'm filled with the Spirit today"?

Rev. John Thomas, the Welsh evangelist, delighted in telling this quaint, homespun parable. Three men were sitting on a wall—Fact, Faith, and Feeling. Feeling slipped and fell and pulled Faith down with him. But Fact remained steadfast; nothing could shake him. In time he reached down and pulled up Faith, who in turn helped Feeling to climb back up.

The interpretation of the parable is this. If we allow our faith to depend on our feelings, then as our feelings go down, faith will also be dragged down. But if we make our faith depend upon fact, upon the truth of God's Word, then nothing can shake it. In fact, the tendency is to help stabilize our feelings as well. The promises of God are the only safe foundation for our faith.

There will also be the temptation to allow our faith to depend on outer manifestations and signs. We may be led to believe that because we do not possess a particular gift of the Spirit therefore we do not possess the Holy Spirit himself. But as we have already pointed out, there are various spiritual gifts and the Holy Spirit reserves the right to distribute them according to His will. Each one of us does not receive all the gifts, nor do we all receive the same gift. We cannot dictate to the Holy Spirit how He shall manifest himself in our lives. That is His prerogative. We should each one receive in gratitude the gift that He offers us, and then unitedly use all these gifts for the edification of the Church and the salvation of sinners.

When I was pastor of an urban, English-speaking church in south India, there were several elderly shut-ins who were members of the congregation. It was my custom to visit them in their homes, read a portion of Scripture, and pray. Many times I took my accordion along and sang one of the old, familiar hymns of the Church. But there were times when it was inconvenient to take my accordion, so I didn't play and sing. Now it would have been ridiculous for one of the shut-ins to say, "Mr. Seamands didn't come to my home today, because he didn't bring his accordion and sing." The important thing was my presence in the home, not that I played an instrument and sang a hymn. In the same way, the manner in which the Holy Spirit manifests himself is not as important as the basic fact of the reality of His presence in our lives.

Sometimes Christians are prone to doubt simply because they feel the tug of temptation in their lives. They fail to distinguish between temptation and sin, and think that, because they are tempted, therefore they have sinned. But temptation itself is not sin. It is only yielding to temptation that produces sin. If temptation itself were sin, then we would be forced to acknowledge that Jesus himself sinned, for He was often sorely tempted. But the Word tells us that He was in every respect tempted as we are, yet *He did not sin* (Heb. 4:15). We will never reach the stage in this life where we will be immune from temptation. As long as we are in this world we shall be tempted and tried. Even the greatest of saints have their temptations.

The important question is, How do we face temptation? What do we do, for example, when feelings of jealousy or resentment begin to arise? Do we harbor them in our hearts and allow them to develop, or do we immediately plead for cleansing and find victory over them? What do we do when lustful thoughts creep into our minds through the eye-gate, as we suddenly view a sensual billboard along the highway, or a sexy advertisement on television? Do we allow them to lodge in our minds and begin to meditate and enlarge upon them? Or by the aid of the Holy Spirit do we immediately cast these thoughts out of our minds? We are not responsible for such thoughts entering our minds from the outside, but we are responsible for receiving them and making them our own. As Martin Luther used to say, "We cannot prevent the birds from flying overhead, but we can certainly prevent them from building a nest in our hair."

There may be an occasion when some temptation catches us off guard and gets the best of us. Does this mean that we have completely lost our relationship to Christ or the presence of the Holy Spirit? Should we give up our faith and deny our whole Christian experience? No. The Holy Spirit is not like a policeman peeking around the corner to catch us in some violation of divine law. He doesn't walk off and leave us at the least deviation from His will. Jesus said that the Holy Spirit comes to abide forever (John 14:16). He comes, not as a transient guest, but as a permanent Resident.

It is the Spirit's intention to stay. Whenever we slip from the path or grieve Him in any way, He instantly checks us and convicts us of our sin. Our immediate response should be that of penitence and obedience. If we have wronged someone, we ought to seek reconciliation and restore the relationship as quickly as possible. If we have been unwittingly caught in a transgression, we should confess our sin immediately and ask His forgiveness. Then we shall find him "faithful and just to forgive us our sins, and to cleanse us from all unrighteousness" (I John 1:9, KJV). Our relationship to God will remain intact.

However, if our sin is a calculated, premeditated one, we grieve the Spirit out of our lives. If we neglect the repeated promptings of the Spirit and allow some barrier to persist between us and our fellowmen or between us and God, then in time we will crowd out the Spirit. His presence will not longer be ours.

The sanctified life is not a state of sinless perfection. We never arrive at a stage where it is impossible to sin. In his magnificent First Epistle, the Apostle John, after declaring unequivocally that "the blood of Jesus his Son cleanses us from all sin," and after clearly exhorting us to refrain from sin, then goes on to say, "But if any one does sin, we have an advocate with the Father, Jesus Christ the righteous" (I John 1:5—2:2). In other words, John implies that even after sanctification it is possible to sin. In such cases, he assures us, Jesus stands ever ready as our Advocate to plead our cause.

However, we must never use this provision as an easy excuse for sin, or for rationalizing questionable conduct. This is an emergency arrangement, not a license for promiscuous living. We don't keep a spare tire in the trunk of the car just so that we may have a puncture. We keep it there just in case we do have a puncture or blowout. We hope we will never need the spare tire, but we feel safe with it on hand. Likewise, God has provided a way of escape for His children who go astray. This is our constant comfort and assurance. But His intention is for us to remain always in the way. The norm is victory, not defeat.

Thus by maintaining an attitude of surrender and obedience, and by keeping our faith grounded on God's Word, we can walk constantly in the Spirit and know the joy and power of His presence. Each day becomes more glorious and meaningful as we continue our earthly pilgrimage with Him.

9

Is This the Answer?

Is Pentecost restricted to dark cloisters and ivory towers or is it related to the marketplace, the campus, the home, the major issues of life? Is it real? Is it relevant? Is it revolutionary?

We need not theorize about the matter. God himself has given us the answer to these questions in the manifestations of His presence and power on numerous occasions of revival and spiritual renewal. The most recent of such outpourings was the visitation of the Spirit upon the campus of Asbury College, which subsequently spread to hundreds of college campuses and churches across the nation. God spoke clearly and decisively.

I shall long remember that eventful day of Feb. 3, 1970, when God manifested himself in great power. My wife and I were having lunch when suddenly our daughter, Sandy, burst into the room. "You simply wouldn't *believe* what's happening at the college," she exclaimed excitedly, as she flung her coat on a chair. "I want to eat lunch in a hurry and go back. I can't stay away!"

"What is happening?" we asked. "You're half an hour late."

My wife and I listened eagerly as Sandy, a sophomore in the college, told the story. That morning the student body had filed into Hughes Auditorium for the regular 10 a.m. chapel service. Instead of the usual song, prayer, and sermon, the period was given over to voluntary testimonies. Anyone who so desired could stand and relate to his college mates what God was doing in his life. As several students witnessed to fresh, personal encounters with Jesus Christ, others began to recognize the spiritual needs in their own lives. An unusual awareness of the Spirit's presence prevailed throughout the entire auditorium.

It soon became evident that the service was an extraordinary one. Fifteen minutes before the end of the chapel period, one of the professors walked up onto the platform and expressed a feeling that opportunity should be given for prayer at the altar. Immediately a number of students responded; soon others followed. By now the atmosphere was electrified. There was a spirit of expectancy in the air.

As the students found spiritual victory at the altar, many of them went up to the pulpit and used the microphone to express their praise to God for His forgiveness and grace. Some made open confession of their sin and hypocrisy; others confessed hidden feelings of resentment and hostility; still others expressed their new-felt joy through song. Here and there throughout the auditorium there were tender scenes of reconciliation as old enmities were melted away by the fervent love of God.

What began as a routine chapel service on that February morning turned out to be the longest and perhaps the most significant chapel service in the 80-year history of Asbury College. It ended exactly one week later. Meanwhile all classes were cancelled, and Hughes Auditorium continued to be the center of activity. By the second morning the revival had crossed the street to its sister institution, Asbury Theological Seminary. Townspeople from Wilmore were starting to attend, and visitors from other states were beginning to arrive. During the hours of daylight as many as

1,200 persons gathered in the auditorium; during the night hours there were never less than 50 to 75 people present. On Sunday the attendance grew to 1,500. All during these days there was no preaching—only praying at the altar, singing, and witnessing.

Soon news of the "marathon revival" began to spread throughout Kentucky and across the nation. The *Lexington Leader* and *Louisville Times* both carried front-page reports with pictures. Station WLEX of Lexington ran a three-minute film clip on the revival during its evening telecast. Newsman Bill Thompson introduced the report by commenting that nothing in his 34 years of newscasting had impressed him as much as the Asbury story. Later on, leading newspapers like the *Indianapolis Star, Chicago Tribune,* and *St. Louis Post-Dispatch* also carried editorials and reports on the movement.

As a result of all this publicity, hundreds of pastors and numerous college officials began to phone in requesting student-teams to come and share the story with their congregations and student bodies. Every Saturday for the next several weeks, a large procession of cars left Wilmore, headed for all points of the compass. Many students traveled by air to distant assignments. By the end of May, approximately 1,500 witness teams had gone out on missions from Asbury College alone, not to mention numerous teams from Asbury Theological Seminary. They ministered on almost 140 college campuses and held services in several thousand churches in practically every state of the Union and even in Canada. Two seminary couples traveled to Colombia, South America, during the spring vacation, and witnessed to missionaries and national church leaders in 25 different gatherings.

In a few instances, the students' testimonies sparked an unusual, spontaneous revival that lasted for days and influenced the entire community. In the Meridian Street Church of God at Anderson, Ind., revival services continued every night for 50 days. People from all over the city filled the sanctuary nightly. In South Pittsburg, Tenn., revival broke out among the students of the local high school. It was estimated that perhaps 500 out of the entire student body of 700 made commitments to Jesus Christ.

As one looks back over the events which followed that initial outpouring at Asbury, one thing stands out clearly. That is the "given-ness" of the revival movement. Though there are evidences of certain human factors that prepared the soil for revival, namely, the spirit of prayer and expectant faith in the hearts of a concerned nucleus of Christian young people, this revival was definitely not the result of human manipulation. It was a "divine happening." God acted sovereignly and graciously. Most of us were taken by surprise. Even outside visitors and secular newsmen who came to observe the event said in awe, "This is God's doing!"

What was God's purpose in all this? Was he trying to say something to us as a people?

I believe there is something significant about the timing of this revival. The decade of the sixties was an explosive decade. It was a period of violence, with strikes, demonstrations, riots, burnings, and assassinations. It was a sordid decade, obsessed with the bizarre and unseemly, when "situation ethics" and free love held sway. It was a period of racial animosity, characterized by white prejudice and black power. The close of the decade left us exhausted, frustrated, and despondent. Was there any hope for the future?

Then suddenly, at the dawning of the seventies, God stepped into the picture. He visited His people. He demonstrated His power. He poured out His love. True, He manifested himself only to isolated portions of the country, but is not God trying to press home a point to the entire nation? Is He not trying to tell us that we have tried every way but the right way—that He has a way to lead us out of our mess? I have a strange feeling that He is.

It is breathtaking to analyze the characteristics of this God-given movement.

A Youth Revival

Many of the young people of our land are in trouble. They have given themselves to demonstrations and violence, to booze and pot, to crime and sex. For them life has no meaning, the future no hope. Then suddenly God became real to a group of college young people. They found a new purpose in life, a new joy in living. Fired with enthusiasm, they committed themselves to a cause far beyond their own resources.

I heard a student in Indiana say to a large congregation, "It's really groovy to be high on the Lord, to be tanked up with the Holy Spirit. It's great, man, it's great!"

Several young people who had become enslaved by drugs and pills found glorious deliverance through the power of the Holy Spirit. One 20-year-old student from Miami, Fla., said to a news reporter of the *Louisville Courier-Journal,* "I had taken trips on everything before coming here; drugs, sex, booze, gambling—everything. I was smoking joints [marijuana] like they were going out of style. Now I don't need to get 'high' on drugs or booze. With drugs you get 'high' and then come down hard. With Christ, I'm going to try to stay on an even keel and try to get all my friends to do the same."

A high school senior in Tennessee said to the entire student body gathered in their assembly: "I've finally found what I've been looking for all this time; not in all this other stuff—sex and booze and drugs—but in Christ."

Through the revival was not God trying to teach us that in the power of His Spirit He has the answer to Youth's problems of today?

An Ethical Revival

During the past decade we witnessed an appalling moral sag in our nation, a decline in basic integrity and in common decency. We heard much about the "credibility gap" and "situation ethics." The double standard was in vogue; divorce reached an all-time mark.

The recent revival produced a renewal of Christian ethics. Students confessed to turning in false reading reports. Some husbands confessed to cheating on their wives. Several employees made restitution for stolen articles. I heard one young man say, as he arose from the altar, "This commitment is going to cost me several hundred dollars. I must set things right." The editor of a newspaper in an Indiana city told the congregation that he would no longer accept advertisements for X-rated movies. A man who was running a liquor store in Tennessee quit the business. A couple who had operated a strip-tease nightclub in San Antonio, Tex., for 17 years closed down the "joint" and placed over the front door this sign: "Closed forever. We have decided to follow Jesus. See you in church Sunday."

A certain congregation will probably never forget the confession of a man in his mid-fifties who stood before the microphone and said, "I have been an active church member for years. I have directed many summer youth camps, but I've been a phony." Then he went on to relate how in the new reorganization of schools in the city he had been so hostile to certain members of the school board that out of spite he had placed dead skunks in their mailboxes and smeared red paint on their driveways. When the Holy Spirit convicted him of his meanness, he went to each one of the homes and confessed that he was the culprit. In the first home the elderly couple broke down and wept. In the second home the husband said angrily, "I threatened to shoot the man if I ever found him out. I feel like shooting you now."

Later he mellowed and expressed admiration for the man's courage in confessing.

The answer to our moral problem is found in the holiness of God and the transforming power of Jesus Christ.

A REVIVAL OF THE CHURCH

The Church has been the target of much criticism in recent years. It has been called "irrelevant," "out-of-date," "out of touch," "a dead organization," "a social club with an ivory-tower mentality," and so on. Much of the criticism is justified. The Church, in many places, is indeed lifeless and impotent.

But as hundreds of young people from many college campuses went out to share their faith with the people, dozens of churches across the country suddenly became alive. These students were talking about a personal encounter with God, how God had delivered them from their "hang-ups" and "turned them on." Their witness had the ring of reality.

Pastors and people responded. The sermon and order of service were pushed aside for the moment. Many church members, tired of pretending for so long, took off their masks and exposed their hypocrisy and phoniness. Broken in spirit, they confessed, prayed, and shared together. Church altars which for years had been nothing more than pieces of furniture now became hallowed places where men met God and brother was reconciled to brother. The usual stiffness and formality gave way to a new freedom in the Spirit. People forgot about the clock and food. They sat for hours in the sanctuary, basking in the presence of God.

An elderly lady in a large church in Atlanta stood, and lifting her hands in the air, prayed, "Lord, thank You for saving us from the sin of sophistication." The pastor of a leading church of another denomination in the same city cried out in prayer, "O God, You have done more in one moment than we have done in five years." A business man, on seeing the Spirit at work and sensing the new feeling of Christian fellowship, said excitedly, "This is the New Testament Church!"

Talk about an ecumenical movement! This was it! The revival cut across all denominational barriers. It spread to "old line" churches steeped in formalism, to evangelical churches whose altars had grown cold. Witnessing knew no bounds of creed. Denominational labels were incidental. The pastor of a church in Robinson, Ill., testified that he saw Presbyterians, Episcopalians, and United Methodists all kneeling together at the altar. Businessmen of several denominations met together each noon for a time of prayer and sharing in the city hall during the revival movement in Anderson, Ind. Everywhere the revival reached, there was a marvelous sense of unity in the Spirit.

Is not God demonstrating to us these days that the Church is still the body of Christ, that it can be gloriously renewed by His Spirit, and that it can once again be an instrument of redemption and reconciliation in the world? Is He not trying to teach us that, without the vitality and purity of the Church, organic unity by itself is inadequate?

A Revival of Mission

In recent years there has been a perceptible sag in the missionary outreach of the American church. Many theologians are questioning our right to evangelize and convert the followers of other religions. Many congregations are wondering if the day of foreign missions is past. Fewer young people are offering themselves for service abroad.

The Asbury revival was a remarkable demonstration of the words of Jesus, "You shall receive power when the Holy Spirit has come upon you; and you shall be my witnesses . . ." As students received a new touch of the Spirit, they felt impelled to share their newfound joy with others. They began phoning their families, friends, and pastors to tell them the "good news."

A call went out to Newsman Paul Harvey, Senator Mark Hatfield, and to a close aide of President Nixon. One girl phoned Madalyn Murray O'Hair, perhaps the nation's best-known atheist, and witnessed to her about God's love and power.

The Holy Spirit could not be contained within the city limits of tiny Wilmore. Soon students and faculty members were fanning out across many states to carry the torch of revival. Many who were previously shy and self-conscious, afraid to speak in public, broke through to new confidence and freedom in the Spirit, and boldly testified to the redemptive power of the risen Lord. One college student flew to Azusa College in California, another to Seattle Pacific College in Washington state. A team went to Oral Roberts University in Tulsa, Okla. Others went to college campuses, home churches, and gatherings in many of the eastern states. One group crossed over into Canada.

In each place they witnessed there was the same response—confession, prayer, testimony, singing, reconciliation. Then, in turn, these groups started going out to surrounding cities to share their newfound victory and joy. Meridian Street Church in Anderson, Ind., alone sent out witness teams to 31 states and to Canada. As a result, thousands upon thousands of people made new commitments to Jesus Christ.

A student from Azusa College in California called on the Sirhan home in the Los Angeles area and for an hour and a half shared with the mother and brother of Robert Kennedy's assassin his witness of the love of Christ.

An Asbury Seminary student went to the Fulton County jail in Atlanta and preached to the prisoners. Out of the 97 men who voluntarily gathered in the chapel, 80 responded to the challenge to accept Christ as personal Savior.

When two student pastors related the story of the revival in a large church in Atlanta, there was a great response from the congregation and many came to the altar for prayer. Three young men received a call to missionary service. When one of the men went home and told his wife about the call, she was quite upset. She said, "Honey, this is one time you'll have to go it alone. I'm not one of God's children and don't intend to be a minister's wife." However, she accompanied her husband to the evening service, and when the invitation was given, she went forward and surrendered herself to Christ. She then went to the microphone, confessed what she had said to her husband in the morning, and went on to say, "Now I am a child of God and I'm on the team with my husband."

I was present at the chapel service in Asbury College on the morning of March 7. The missionary dimension of the revival was much in evidence. President Kinlaw told of receiving a letter from Colombia, South America, asking for some college students to come down during the summer and hold meetings among the youth. "I don't know where the money will come from," he remarked, "but it will have to come from this side."

A seminary professor called from the balcony, "I would like the privilege of giving the first $100." Then a professor from the college made a pledge of $250. A student walked to the platform and told how his witness team had received an offering of $200 the previous weekend. "Our group would like the amount to go to this missionary project," he said. An attractive coed stood up and said, "Here's a $10.00 bill I was planning to spend on a new skirt this afternoon." Then someone suggested an offering basket be placed on the platform. Before the chapel service ended, over $1,000 had been collected for the mission. Later the total increased to over $2,000. As a result, a group of college students went down to Colombia that summer, ministering in the name of Christ.

God's cure for the missionary slump in American churches is a fresh outpouring of the Holy Spirit upon the people of God. He alone is the Originator and Promoter of Christian missions.

A Revival of Love

How much bitterness, hatred, and violence we witnessed in the decade of the sixties, between "doves" and "hawks," blacks and whites, student body and administration, labor and management! It was the decade of the clenched fist and the sharp tongue.

The secular newspapers spoke of the Asbury revival as a great "love-in." They were right. God gave His people a new baptism of love. Resentments were exposed, jealousies cleansed; hostilities melted away. As people were reconciled to God, they were reconciled to their fellowman. It was a common sight to see someone stand in the congregation, call out the name of a person seated there, ask forgiveness, and then to see the two meet in the aisle and embrace. Often husbands and wives, holding hands, walked down the aisle and knelt together at the altar, or stood behind the pulpit, with arms around each other, and spoke of their newfound love for God and for one another. I saw a most beautiful sight when I peeked into the seminary chapel late one afternoon. The pews were empty, but the altar was filled with young married couples kneeling together in prayer and jointly making new commitments to God.

This was no sentimental emotion or momentary effervesence. This was the love of God "poured into our hearts through the Holy Spirit." In church after church the atmosphere was charged with love.

When an African student who is studying at Asbury College went to a church in Ohio to tell the story of the revival and give his personal testimony, spontaneously several members of the congregation stepped forward and put their arms around him as an expression of their love. Kneeling beside a businessman in an Indiana church, I heard him pray through tears, "Lord I thank You for making it possible for me to love the colored folk and many people who were so obnoxious to me before. Now I feel I can love everybody."

When revival broke out in South Pittsburg, Tenn., the small sanctuary of the church where the meetings were being held soon became inadequate for the overflow crowds. Someone suggested they move the services to a large church which was located in the same block. But this posed a problem. Many Negro students were attending the services each evening, and so far the congregation of this big church had not opened its doors to the blacks. But God's Spirit broke down all barriers. The minister very graciously offered his church for the rest of the week and announced over the radio that there would be perfect freedom for all to attend. He even contacted three of the leading Negro citizens in town and made it clear that the blacks were welcome.

It was this atmosphere of love that helped to bridge the "generation gap" also. New lines of communication were opened up between parent and child, between adult and teen-ager. The revival started with the youth and then spread to the adults. Both age-groups listened to and got through to each other. Teen-agers felt they could trust those over 30; the elderly felt they could learn something from the adolescent. Age no longer seemed a barrier. People forgot who was old and who was young. One moment a youth in his twenties would be sharing his testimony at the microphone; the next, a gray-haired old man; followed by a schoolgirl in her early teens. In a large rally in Anderson, Ind., where 2,000 people were present, a hippie with full beard and shoulder-length hair received Christ as his Saviour and gave a witness before the whole congregation. An 80-year-old grandmother, with snow-white hair done up in a bun, went forward and hugged him!

God is trying to teach us that the only answer to our racial strife, the generation gap, and our national divisions is His divine love operating within us. He is offering to us the gift of His Spirit, the only One who can make us on tiptoe with love.

What Pigs Can Teach Us About Parenting

In pig

Three is a significant number when it comes to pig gestation. As a rule of thumb, from the moment of conception, it takes a sow three months, three weeks and three days for a pregnancy to come full term. When I first learned about this during my time as an overwhelmed keeper of pigs, it struck me as being quite magical and continues to do so now. I had no desire to increase the pig count in my garden – quite the opposite, in fact – but I still think of this means of counting down towards the arrival of a litter as a form of poetry.

The nesting instinct

Maybe I just wasn't paying enough attention when we did the traditional primary school trip to the farm. Perhaps I'd left the room to put the kettle on when they covered it in the natural world documentaries. Whatever the case, it's only recently that I realised I have drifted through life without ever coming across the quite wonderful fact that pigs are masters in the craft of building nests.

I've always known that birds don't have the monopoly here. Mammals from the mouse to the gorilla are known to spin together a nice, safe space to sleep or raise their young. When Professor Mendl tells me that pigs belong to the same exclusive club, my first response is to pretend I knew this all along and hope he doesn't see through me.

'In the wild, if you know what to look for you'll find wild boar nests,' he says, and, frankly, if I wasn't so intimidated by these animals I would head straight out and look for some. 'Generally, piglets stay with their mother in a structure like this for the first week. Then they start to venture out.'

The Professor tells me that nest building is a form of functional behaviour, for domestic pigs as much as wild boar, in that it serves a specific purpose. If she's free to create such a structure, the expectant sow is able to isolate herself from the group in an environment that feels protected, safe and warm. We talk about the evolution of the farrowing crate, which is a box used in industrial pig farming that allows the mother just enough space to lie down to give birth without crushing the piglets. In doing so, I begin to understand how important the Professor's work is in constantly striving to improve pig welfare. The nest is a home woven by the occupant to meet their needs exactly. We might be able to create an artificial space in the name of grand-scale efficiency, but the ultimate aim must be to encourage that nesting instinct and allow pigs the pleasure and satisfaction that comes from any self-build.

When I raise the subject of pig nesting with Wendy on her farm, she tells me that it isn't just reserved for the sow preparing to farrow.

'Oh, I've seen boys building nests,' she says quite casually. We're standing at the edge of her courtyard now, taking turns with a hose to wash down our wellingtons. I've already had one go, but it's going to take several attempts to properly clean them. 'Pigs are just clever at building something warm and cosy, where they can sleep.'

'What does it look like?' I ask, having come clean about the fact that I only learned about their crafting skills during my conversation with the Professor.

Wendy hands me the hose again.

'Like a giant bird's nest,' she says. 'If a sow is about to have piglets, she'll spend 24 hours building it. During that time she'll take anything: buckets, hosepipes, brushes – whatever she can drag. It's just her instinct to dig a hollow and then pile anything into a big bowl shape.'

By now, I am itching to see an example. Wendy tells me she hasn't come across one for a while, which just makes them seem even more mythical in my mind.

'Are some pigs better than others at nest building?' I ask.

'The Swedes are unbelievably good at it,' says Wendy, in a moment of rare praise for the breed. I want to ask her if they build them from a flat pack, but decide to keep that to myself. 'They tend to collect stuff around four in the afternoon, often when it starts to get cooler and darker in the winter months. They'll go up into the woods, find a bloody great big branch and drag it out. And then I'll hear an almighty rumpus because they can't fit it into their ark. So, they have to abandon it and find something smaller.'

'So, the nest building doesn't always happen out in the open?' I ask, because something here has struck a note with me.

When Wendy confirms that she often finds nests inside the pig's sleeping quarters, I realise that I have seen plenty without realising.

A magpie in the house

During their early residence inside our house, Butch and Roxi tested me in many different ways. As they were Emma's pet project, I hadn't envisaged that I'd have much to do with them. Then the first day of the week arrived and I found myself in the role of writer and sole carer to a pair of tiny, squeaking pigs that seemed really pleased to be in my company.

In some ways, the house went to ruin as much as my work throughout this time. If I wasn't scrubbing the carpet in the corner of the front room I was banging extra nails into the floorboards to stop them from being uprooted. The fridge was another flashpoint, in that I couldn't attempt to make a sandwich for lunch without Roxi staging a drama. But perhaps Butch was responsible for the greatest test of all, and that took the form of thieving.

In a busy household, things are always going missing. Socks end up in the wrong drawer, and go on rotation from one bedroom to another, while the kids almost always wait until we're heading out for school to declare that they've mislaid their PE kit. I'm used to putting stuff down and then finding it gone. Living under the same roof as Butch, I found I couldn't even put that thing down, because it would be missing in the first place.

It wasn't just the frequency with which things disappeared. The items our boar stole seemed both random and baffling. In a typical week, I could lose everything from the insole of a shoe to a towel from the rail in the bathroom, my hole puncher and the tongs for the wood burner. Naturally, in the beginning, I blamed the youngest of my children. My poor son was accused of wandering off with a box of plasters, the kitchen apron and a recipe card for paella. He also received a grovelling apology when I found all the items rammed inside Butch and Roxi's little pig ark.

'What does he think he is?' I asked Emma one time, having searched the house for a phone charger and then found it in what had become a robbers' lock-up. 'A minipig or a magpie?'

All this occurred at a time before they trashed the house and then went on to become a growing responsibility in my garden. As far as Emma was concerned, I was just moaning because I had yet to bond with Butch and Roxi as she had, and then fill my social media feed with improbable pictures of the pair.

'It's just stuff,' she reasoned. 'Nothing precious.'

A few days later, she changed her tune, but not the channels on the TV, when Butch stole the remote. It was one of the kids who bellowed that it was missing, and me who conducted a search of the pig ark in my office. Sure enough, I found it among the Lego bricks and pens. Of all the things my family couldn't function without, I thought to myself on returning it to the front room, it was this. He could've taken the car keys or my wallet, but the TV remote was a step too far.

'Here.' I tossed the remote to Emma and then addressed the kids as they stopped panicking and ceased turning the house upside down. 'In future, if you want to keep anything safe in this house, place it at least three feet off the ground so the pigs can't reach it.'

This wasn't the kind of advice I had ever imagined I would share with my children, but they certainly took it on board when their mother tutted and drew our attention to the remote in her hand.

'Look at it,' she said, though a moment passed before I realised what was wrong. '*Look at the buttons!*'

I am guessing that Butch was drawn by the scent of all those fingertips searching the channels for something decent to watch. Having dragged the remote into the straw, he must've just got carried away and nibbled pretty much all of them down to nubs. The remote was useless, and life in our house transformed beyond recognition until the replacement arrived a few days later. That was the moment Butch earned everyone's forgiveness, but it wasn't until I spent time with people who truly understood pigs that I realised his true motive.

'He was nest building,' says Wendy with absolute conviction when I tell her the story. 'If you give a pig a chance, you'll always find something in amongst the straw.'

The mothering instinct

If both male and female pigs are instinctively skilled in creating nests, only the expectant mothers do so in preparation for the arrival of their young. Given their skills as homemakers, I ask Professor Mendl if the boar shows any interest in antenatal care.

'It's a good question,' he says with a half-smile, and I can tell as he looks to a point midway between us that he'd like to respond with a list of all the things they do to support the mother. A moment later, having found nothing to report, it seems, the Professor blinks and returns his attention to me.

'I suppose defending behaviour would make sense if such a situation arose,' he offers finally, 'but the boar don't provide in any way, the mother does everything.'

From the moment a piglet arrives in this world, weighing just a couple of pounds, it relies on strong guiding signals. While the sow tends to lie on her side for the first few days, she serves as a command centre for her brood as much as a source of life. With litters numbering on average between eight and 12, the piglet quite literally faces a fight for survival. Firstly, piglets are poorly insulated. They must huddle to stay warm, both with each other and by staying close to their mother in the nest. Piglets also shiver to achieve the same effect, and critically, they have to suckle in order to thrive, as well as receiving antibodies in the milk that are vital to boosting immunity. Led by the smell from the mother's teats, they follow the direction of her bristles. Like a signposting of the senses, these grow in such a way as to take the sow's newborns to the source. Here, the piglet and her hungry brothers and sisters overcome a scene of potential chaos every feeding time and achieve something extraordinary.

Smart suckling

'Teat order is set up soon after birth,' Professor Mendl tells me. 'Calling upon odour cues from the sow and whoever is next to them, each piglet claims a teat. There's usually a bit of pushing and shoving to begin, and it must be challenging for the ones in the middle, but eventually the order emerges and they settle down.'

Known as 'teat fidelity', this established system holds true throughout the suckling period. The Professor goes on to explain that the teats towards the front of the sow produce more milk than those at the back, which is often where the weakest will end up. The runt, as we often call the unlucky piglet, may well have been the last to be born. It's a cruel outcome based on chance, but begins to school the piglets in vital life lessons. In the time it takes for them each to settle on a teat, they've come to recognise the importance of a social hierarchy as much as the benefits of working as a group. Meantime, the mother has barely begun to school them.

'In the wild, she'll suckle them for between eight and 12 weeks,' says Professor Mendl. 'On farms they can be weaned at one month, and in that period the mother is the most important pig of all to them.' He explains that the sow produces milk approximately once an hour, but in order for the milk to be let down, the piglets must stimulate her teats. 'The mother will grunt to her offspring in a particular way to indicate when it's time for them to latch on, which means the piglets quickly learn to respond to her voice,' he

continues. 'They'll massage the teats for up to 15 minutes, before she tells them that the milk is on the way, and then everything is synchronised so that all the piglets get their milk at the same time.'

I am surprised to learn that this drinking phase only lasts for up to a minute, during which time the mother's grunting can become lower and softer in tone. Some have observed that it sounds a little like she's singing to her young, but it's believed that in fact she's providing a kind of running commentary. In return, once that milk drop is over, the young will continue to knead her teats as a means of reporting back with a nutritional update – with more kneading serving as a request for a bigger drop next time, and less for a reduction. It's an intensely close bond, and one that enables the mother to be certain that she is providing to the best of her abilities. In the wild, she also relies on her young to notify her when they are ready to be weaned. 'As they grow older, the piglets will massage less,' says

Professor Mendl, 'and so gradually the milk production begins to dry up.'

The other mothers

The mother will remain a central influence on her piglets once she's rejoined the group with them. Even so, the youngsters will pick up on vital survival skills from the other members. In effect, the group will teach them how to dig, work out what's good to eat, resolve differences and acquire all the tools they need to effectively become a good pig.

'It's mainly the sows that teach the young to forage,' says Wendy. 'If I hand-rear piglets, then I can have a hell of a job getting them to eat naturally. I can put anything on the floor, but unless it's Frosties – which they love – they'll just ignore it. I have to put food raised up on bricks before they'll even show an interest, whereas a piglet that's been on the teat will be taught to forage within 10 days.'

I love the fact that the sow relies on her sisters in the group to help raise and educate her young. In this matrilineal structure, each new generation is effectively mothered on a communal level. This is the glue that bonds each group, providing a secure environment for the young males to find their feet and ultimately strike out independently, while forging strong ties between the females that can last a lifetime.

Of course, piglets also learn a great deal from each other, as Professor Mendl explains. 'Certain actions are intrinsically rewarding for pigs,' he begins. 'Just like it is with humans, one of those actions is play. There is evidence that when animals like pigs are playing it causes a change in brain chemistry. In this case, the reward may drive the behaviour.'

So, what looks like frolics, fun and games is in fact an experience for the piglet that's as enjoyable as it is enlightening, and brings them back for more. Play between the piglet and its brothers and sisters can begin from three weeks and grow until they're interacting with each other more than they are with the adult sows. But while the rest of the group will watch out for the piglets, it's their mother who makes every sacrifice for them. Ultimately, her sense of nurture and protection knows no bounds.

'A sow would kill to protect her young,' Wendy tells me. 'When there are little piglets around she can be very aggressive towards you, but mostly I am struck by their commitment to nursing. Sometimes during this time their teats can get ripped to shreds. The little ones might be arguing over the teats, and pulling or biting and generally being really naughty, and that poor mother is just lying there and feeding them. Occasionally, she'll roll onto her tummy and shout "Enough!" and will only let them feed again when everything is calm. But the fact is no matter what the circumstances, those piglets are always fed.'

'Do they respect their mother?' I ask, thinking that if I let my kids scramble for food at the table they would be feral in no time.

'Oh, yes!' says Wendy. 'I have seen a sow chuck a piglet in the air with her snout if it's misbehaving. She doesn't interfere with the fights when they're little, because they have to establish their own pecking order, but there is always discipline within the group.'

The spare-part parent

Having had just one job so far, I'm curious about the role of the boar during this nurturing phase. What part do they play as the piglets grow in size as much as confidence, and wake up to their place in the world? Despite doing nothing to help during the pregnancy, does the father have an input in raising his young or is it all down to the sows?

Professor Mendl tells me the boar is very 'spare-partish' as a parent, and I judge from his tone that he's being kind. When I ask Wendy, even she thinks long and hard before answering.

'Well, they are nice to them,' she says diplomatically. 'They'll certainly protect piglets. There is an instinct there to do that. He'll sleep in a huddle with the piglets and the sows in the group, and if anything disturbs them, he will act. I suppose the younger boars might copy his behaviour to a certain degree, but that's where it ends,' she tells me, before stressing how important it is as a pig-keeper to separate the boar from the youngsters before they become sexually mature. In a way, this just serves to foreground the boar's primary role, while highlighting the fact that the greatest formative influence for all young pigs are the females in their lives.

Sybil

'She was a sow who produced my first litter. It was an amazing experience, but also a story about survival.' Wendy turns off the hose we have been using. Our boots are clean and glistening wet, but rather than head back inside the farmhouse we remain in the courtyard. It's a beautiful day, and it feels like a rarity after the weather we've had. 'I can't describe the feeling when I saw Sybil for the first time,' she continues. 'She was a tiny piglet just toddling around, and we grew really close. I was really excited when she fell pregnant as an adult sow, and knew she'd be an amazing mother. But soon after she gave birth, Sybil fell sick.'

Wendy hesitates, having told me this. All of a sudden, her eyes start to shine. 'The vet said she must have torn something inside, and so all we could do was dose her with penicillin and hope for the best. And do you know what? For the next three weeks that pig dragged herself through so much suffering just to nurse her young. I swear she kept herself alive just to get them over the cusp so that they could survive on their own.' A catch in her voice stops Wendy once more, and she takes a moment to compose herself.

'I was in with her just before the end, but I really wasn't prepared for her to go,' she continues. 'I held her trotter and promised that I would look after her piglets for her, and she just slipped away. My only regret was that I didn't sit with her for long afterwards. I was just so broken, and had to go inside. I left her with her piglets for the day, and was just so sad for them. They stayed to drink her dry and say goodbye, but I was true to my word. I raised them as if I had lost a daughter and been left with her children.'

Striking out

There comes a time in any family structure when the sons or daughters decide to move on. For us as parents, it might be a day we come to dread, or one that finally arrives after endless hints only to discover it also leaves a hole behind that's hard to fill. We might long to hear from our children after they've departed, even though they were always under our feet when we shared the same roof. Whatever the case, it's heartening to see them spread their wings and grow into adults in their own right.

In some ways, pigs have perfected this uneasy transition in a way that suits everyone involved. In the wild, the boys will drift away to form sounders of their own, while other boars may draw some of their sisters from the group. With some of her girls left behind, the sow never experiences that empty nest feeling. She might well fill it to the brim once more by repeating the process all over again, or become a grandmother. As for the domestic pig, it could be said that they have enrolled our help in the separation process to make it as painless as possible.

'I tend to wean the piglets at eight weeks,' says Wendy, describing a commonplace part of livestock management on farms and smallholdings in which the young are switched from teat to solid food. 'If it's a massive litter and exhausting for the mother then I'll do it at six weeks, but if there's only three or four piglets, I might leave them to it for 10 weeks.'

By then, as Wendy points out, the piglets are no longer tiny tots but marauding teenagers with a milk fixation. The key, as she explains, is in separating the mother and her litter with both efficiency and sensitivity. 'Initially, I remove all the young ones so the mother's milk dries up,' she says. 'The female weaners can rejoin her with no problems, but as the boys are approaching sexual maturity I keep them separate.'

'How do the girls respond to each other?' I ask.

Wendy turns her attention to the pigs in the yard.

'It's not so much a mother and daughter bond,' she says after a moment. 'I don't feel like pigs recognise each other as relatives, but there is a companionship which is really important to them. It's about feeling safe,' she suggests, 'being able to curl up together and having someone to talk to.' Wendy falls quiet, still contemplating her pigs, and then nods to herself. 'Aren't those the three things that all of us want in life?'

10
The Companion Pig

Not just for Christmas

Do pigs make good pets? From experience, I would say there is an unbridgeable gap between the fantasy and reality. Pigs are smart and friendly, characterful and gentle. They enjoy your company, make very good listeners and will happily conduct a conversation for as long as you like. Pigs like being scratched and tickled, and if there's a treat involved then no doubt you can teach them tricks. But there is a reason why the cat and the dog are often ranked as the second and third most popular pets in the world, eclipsed inexplicably by the freshwater fish, and why the pig doesn't even feature in the Top 10.

Despite the close relationship between human and animal, the fact is that we live in completely different worlds. It's possible for these worlds to interlink, as Wendy and countless smallholders demonstrate. In fact, anyone with a passion for these deeply rewarding creatures as well as the resources and commitment to their welfare can make it work. Nevertheless, unlike a dog, it has to be said that a pig is not just for life, it's a *way* of life.

For one thing, you need a lot of land. I had no issue in giving up our garden to accommodate Butch and Roxi. That was the price we paid for not doing our research properly. Of course I grumbled on getting out of bed before dawn each morning to feed them, but it had to be done for the sake of our neighbours. It's just that as time passed, and the minipigs turned into maximonsters, it became apparent to us all that everything we could offer them wasn't enough.

Take my composting system. For a period of time, Butch and Roxi produced the perfect amount of dung for me to mix in with the grass clippings from what little lawn we had left. The result was a fertile cocktail that I scattered on my flowerbeds in spring and used as mulch in the autumn. Slowly, however, the delicate balance between dung and clippings began to tip in favour of the former. My compost just became a pile of poo, and with that came a plague of flies. During the warmer months, we couldn't step outside without walking into a malevolent buzzing cloud, while the heap itself slowly towered and teetered unsustainably.

My first plan of action was to salt away what I could, much like some rural version of *The Great Escape*. Rather than drop the dung through my trouser legs as I took the dog for a walk in the woods, I planned to carry a bucket with me and deposit it along the way. Then Emma reminded me that pigs are so carefully controlled by DEFRA that I'd possibly be looking at prison time, and the burning shame of having to tell my cellmates why I was inside. Just as the pile looked set to topple, I found a sympathetic stable owner who lived a short car ride away. He had no problem with me adding my waste to his industrial-sized compost, which could easily accommodate the weekly output from two domestic pigs.

The challenge, I discovered, was in transporting it there.

On our first journey, I pulled up in the car with Emma at my side, both windows open and the pair of us dry-heaving at the wretched stink we had brought with us. We had loaded not just buckets but three black plastic bins, one of which had tipped over in the back when I turned off the lane. Then we had to manhandle our cargo to the heap itself, which stood beyond a sea of slurry that more than engulfed our boots. The upshot was a car that required an industrial clean and a marginally reduced pig-dung pile at home that promptly returned to its former magnificence within a week.

As fast as I dug out their latrine area, Butch and Roxi filled it. In fact, the perimeter of that space they had so carefully created steadily began to grow. Meanwhile, both pigs had dug and turned their enclosure and their emergency extension so comprehensively that it quite possibly shared the same nutrient content as the surface of Mars. I needed to rest both areas in order for it to recover, but the hard truth was I had nothing more to give. Our friendly pig man down the road cut us a break around this time, and offered to take our oversized swine on his fields for a while. We seized upon the opportunity, as did Butch and Roxi – on finding a way out of there that none of his sows had ever previously found.

By then, Emma and I were schooled in pig search and rescue, as were most of the village. It was no longer a novelty, and with the field deemed unsuitable and the pair back in our enclosure we knew that something had to change. A domestic cat or a dog didn't present this much grief on a daily basis. Pigs might have come in from the wild just as those animals did, but as pets, they arrived at a price.

Man's beast friend

So, you can't let a pig curl up in your lap at the end of a long day, and taking one for a stroll with you is not as easy as slipping on a leash. For one thing you need a movement licence. Quite frankly, if walking the dog required doing some paperwork first, our four-legged friend would plunge out of the pet popularity charts quicker than a Christmas novelty song in January.

Having said that, I can fully appreciate why people like Wendy have such a close connection with pigs that they couldn't envisage life without them. They may not be loyal like a dog, preferring the company of their own kind, but it's perfectly possible to share a level of reckoning with a pig. Even when Butch and Roxi travelled beyond the limits of my patience, I always considered them soulful and deeply sensitive animals. We shared a bond – I just didn't have the means to nurture it.

Mindful that in general pigs are raised for the table, which is not something that registers in my life, I turn to Professor Mendl to find out if the pig serves any other useful purpose to us.

'Could they act like guard dogs?' I ask. 'They certainly protected our chickens, because we never had a fox attack on their watch.'

'Wild boar can certainly be dangerous animals,' he says, 'and a domestic pig could serve some alerting function. Then again, a dog can do the same thing, and you can move a dog.'

I still like the idea of recruiting a couple of pigs as patrollers. They are sharp-eared and likely to pick up on any uninvited presence. They can also be intimidatingly big and frankly, terrifying, should they be provoked into squealing. I also recognise that pigs aren't known for coming to heel, just as the Professor points out, and accept that Alsatians everywhere need not worry about their jobs.

I float the idea to Wendy, simply because in telling me stories about Rocky, her huge free-roaming pig, she mentioned that visitors were often persuaded to stay inside their cars on the drive when he trotted round to greet them. Does she feel safer in her farmhouse at night, knowing that the pigs are out there, watching over her?

'No,' she says, quite simply, and brings my little fantasy crashing down. 'Pigs sleep really deeply at night. I can walk around outside in the dark and nobody stirs. They just snore really loudly.'

Across the courtyard, I notice several hens perched on a partition wall between two enclosures. They have plenty of space available to them, no doubt to lay their eggs in peace, and look relaxed in the company of the occupants below. I also don't suppose the foxes are foolish enough to regard Wendy's flock as prey.

'Do the pigs get on well with other animals here?' I ask.

'Oh, they're friends with goats, horses and sheep,' says Wendy. 'I don't see any hierarchy between the species,' she adds. 'If I fed them all together, I might find out who's in charge, and I suspect it would be the sheep.'

'How so?' I ask, and Wendy responds by headbutting the air.

'Oh, I see.'

'The horses can be instinctively scared of pigs,' she says, 'but if you let them get over it, they're fine together. I've even seen them asleep together, and the same goes for pigs and dogs.'

I smile at the thought, and tell her that I'm taken by the idea of the pig as everybody's friend on the farm. I'm still searching my mind for the role that would make a pig invaluable to a human, however, and decide to address the obvious.

'How about truffle hunting?' I ask, for it's believed that these precious underground fungi give off a smell very similar to the animal's sex hormones.

Wendy reacts like she's been waiting for me to ask her this question all this time. 'If I could do that then I'd be rich,' she laughs. While recognising that truffle-hunting pigs are often fruitfully employed on the continent, she tells me that in her experience domestic pigs aren't big on mushrooms and believes this might be down to their heritage in the wild. 'We're switched on about not eating any old mushroom from the woodland because of the risk of poisoning,' she says. 'Pigs are just the same.'

From this hillside farm, with its elevated views, it's possible to watch sunset shadows reach across entire fields. I've had a lovely time in the company of Wendy and her pigs. It really does feel like another world, but I do need to get back to my humdrum reality. Emma is at work, and my children are old enough to survive without me after school. They have my number if they need me, but perhaps more reassuringly, my dogs are there. Neither of them will mediate any arguments or help to cook them tea, and frankly, a clapped-out old rescue mutt and a miniature sausage dog won't do much to stop someone stealing the lawnmower from the shed. Still, I know they're watching over our kids, which brings me back to the concept of pigs as companion animals. Wendy has been astute in helping me to understand what they see in each other, but what does she see in pigs?

'It's what they give back. They appreciate your affections and love you for it,' she says quite clearly. 'I know that's a human expression,' she adds, 'but I really do feel a lot from them, and you get what you put in. Some of my pigs are oblivious to me. They don't give a damn, but when you get a pig like Rocky or Brad, then I put the time and effort into getting to know them. Is it worthwhile?' she asks, taking the question from my lips and then providing an answer I completely understand. 'Oh, I get a *huge* amount in return.'

Pastures new

There is, of course, one role in particular that is perfectly suited for the pig. If there's any truth in the saying that doing a job you love means never having to work again, then Butch and Roxi lucked out on every level.

In short, we found them gainful employment as ground labourers.

Several years after the minipigs arrived in a cat basket, they set off for their new lives in a horsebox. By this time, Butch and Roxi couldn't even be considered to be normal-sized pigs. While Butch was the size of a ridgeback, Roxi stood waist-high to me, measured six feet in length and clocked in at an estimated 25 stone. They had become hogzillas, and despite our best efforts, care and attention, the life we provided them was no longer sufficient for their needs.

Via social media, where she regularly unloaded about life under siege from swine, Emma had connected with a friendly organic sheep farmer in the north of the country. In talking to him, it turned out he was looking for two pigs to turn the soil in an epic way. In an earlier agricultural age, so he told us, pigs were regularly employed to clear rough ground and undergrowth. In his view, they did a more thorough job than machinery, and were more rewarding too. With this in mind, the farmer had plans to grow what he called medicinal fields for his flock, in which sheep could graze on selected grasses and plants that were of specific benefit to their health. It was, in our view, the perfect outcome. Butch and Roxi would have more space than we could ever give them, and an opportunity to provide a useful service rather than racking up repair bills. But first, we had to break it to the family.

Throughout my time as a pig-keeper, I think our kids learned to curse from me. Emma wasn't far behind on the bad language whenever the sound of fence panels could be heard splintering in the enclosure, or that time she returned, having slipped face down in the slurry. For all the grief they caused us, however, the children enjoyed the sunny side of pig-keeping. They would drift down to spend time with Butch and Roxi, and I've no doubt they provided a dependable listening ear. So it was no surprise that they became emotional as I steered the pigs out of the wreckage of their enclosure towards the waiting transport. Emma cried with them, but in view of where they were heading nobody was distraught.

Once everyone had said their farewells, I secured the rear doors of the equine trailer we had borrowed for the day, along with the four-by-four I needed to tow it, and set off with mixed emotions. It was a strange feeling as I drove out into the early light. I felt a huge sense of relief all the way there, and an increasing dread.

Butch and Roxi looked delighted by their new pig ark, and the attention from the farmer and his partner, while the sprawling moorland paddock allocated to them was carpeted in grass and reeds. I knew they would be happy there, and left without making a fuss of them. In our time together, I had come to believe that pigs can pick up on how we're feeling. Just then, despite my cheery farewells with the farmer, I didn't want them to see through me. Butch and Roxi hadn't just become a part of my life, they had formed the axis around which everything revolved. It wasn't sustainable, but I knew that for some time I would be adrift without them. When I finally returned home that night, a little bit of me expected to find them waiting at the back door with a look that questioned why I had taken so long. I even looked around before stepping inside, but they had gone.

If the children remembered anything about that chaotic time, it wasn't the very short period when they could've scooped up Butch and Roxi with one hand. Hopefully, what stuck with them was the effort their parents made to give two maxed-out minibeasts a happy home. Like us, they have also acquired a soft spot for pigs, but that goes no further than remarking on them when passing a farm or if one crops up on TV. The farmer's partner was great at keeping us updated, and I would show the family any pictures she sent of the pigs thriving in their new home. I wasn't sure what to make of the photograph of Butch and Roxi rooting up a field amid a flock of indignant sheep, but we all agreed it was beautifully foregrounded by the smashed remains of a drystone wall.

I still keep chickens at the foot of the garden. They poke and scratch about in the weeds, darting at bugs and waltzing with each other in their own special way, but we all still call it the pig enclosure. Every time I visit them, and see the sleeping quarters at the back of the shed that I now use as storage, I think about those years when a sow and a boar uprooted our lives. It's very quiet down there, a whole lot more peaceful, and frankly, just not the same without them.

Acknowledgements

I should like to thank my editor, Vicky Eribo, for her light touch with the metaphorical pig board. She has guided and steered this book in such a way that I feel like I got there on my own, though in truth I would've been lost without her. I am also very grateful to the entire team at HarperCollins for their support and enthusiasm as well as Philippa Milnes-Smith and all at LAW. My thanks also to Emma, Graham for the help and advice when we needed it and also Butch and Roxi, of course.

Finally, I would like to thank Wendy Scudamore and Professor Michael Mendl for all the qualities embodied in their wonderful contributions to this book, but above all for being great fun. Not only did they give their time, insight and experience into the world of pigs, but both proved to be fascinating, funny, charming and wise. I am grateful to Wendy for parking her fine pig transport business in order to bring me up to speed, and to Professor Mendl for showing me that academic life can be really quite cool. I am also mindful that his work in the field of pig cognition is based on rigorous investigation, and wish to recognise the following work as central to his findings: Mendl, M., Held, S. and Byrne, R. W. (2010): *Current*

Biology 20, R796-798; Held, S., Cooper, J. J. and Mendl, M. (2009): 'Advances in the study of cognition, behavioural priorities and emotions', pp. 47–94 in *The Welfare of Pigs*, ed. J. N. Marchant-Forde (Springer).